PIIA NYKANEN

Rewrite the Stars – How to Use Creative Writing to Overcome Trauma

Copyright © 2018 by Piia Nykanen

All rights reserved. No part of this publication may be reproduced, stored or transmitted in any form or by any means, electronic, mechanical, photocopying, recording, scanning, or otherwise without written permission from the publisher. It is illegal to copy this book, post it to a website, or distribute it by any other means without permission.

First edition

ISBN: 9780987640512

Editing by Megan Whiting

This book was professionally typeset on Reedsy. Find out more at reedsy.com

Contents

Foreword   v
Introduction   vii

I   UNLEASH YOUR CREATIVITY

My story	3
Why write? Finding your way to inspired writing	11
Fear of shedding the mask	15
Awareness of communication - what do writing and creative...	19
Unleash successful content	27
The feeling of vulnerability and sharing your writing	30
Find your champions	36
Journaling ideas	39
Ideas for writing and where to get them	44

II   PRACTICAL SAMPLES FOR INSPIRATION

Point of view - who is telling your story?	51
Travel writing	53
Screenwriting	62
Short stories	70
Symbolism mythology, cultural background and childhood...	84
Lifestyle writing	94
Ready to unleash your writing to the world?	105
Writing competitions and scholarships	109
Creative prompts and practice dialogue	115

III WORKSHEETS

Worksheet 1 - Identify and discover you; examine your habits...   135
Worksheet 2 - Kickstart the creative writing process   137
Worksheet 3 - Observations and writing activities to help...   140
Worksheet 4 - Character inspiration and dialogue practice   142
Final word   144

Foreword

The moment I opened this book, it gave me a good feeling; a feeling of a safe space.

Piia did a fantastic job of writing something that is raw, completely honest and relatable. She told her story of bullying, highlighting the emotional and physical impact it has on the victim. This book shares her encounters with bullying and how turning to creative writing was a positive form of therapy. Creative writing has always been an outlet for me as well and after reading this book, it has driven me to write and share struggles in my life as I now feel more safe and confident to do so after reading about Piia's journey and her courage to share with the world.

Bullied victims often feel alone because they may feel they have nothing to turn to as an escape. Creative writing (as demonstrated in this book) proves to be a positive outlet to unload the burden, offload the negative thoughts and 'brainstorm' ideas, which in return, broadens the mind. Seeing ideas written down may show the victim that they have strengths, skills and knowledge they mightn't have acknowledged. This can lead to confidence and self-recognition to realise that they don't have to absorb what the bullies say to them. I know from experience that if someone has put me down and my head is clouded with negative thoughts that I look forward to picking up a pen and writing. Even if I don't have a story idea, I just start putting words on paper and it doesn't take long to have a new focus; a positive distraction that suddenly doesn't make things seem as bad. If writing hasn't particularly been something that has interested you before, even sitting down for just five to ten minutes can be quite therapeutic.

Throughout the book, Piia has included short stories which were all unique and beautifully written. Her writing captures the reader instantly, making you feel like you are right there in the scene with the character. It is no wonder that her writing has been selected and published in online articles.

Rewrite the Stars certainly does not have a limited audience and has been recommended by schools as a 'must read'. Whether you have been bullied or not, this book relates to anybody, any age, because it promotes positivity in everyday life no matter what your situation is. It also reminds us, that in a world that has become so fast-paced, money driven, and materialistic, to slow down, be kind and appreciate the little things in life.

Natalie Hughes, Author of Fake Escape and Whispered Revenge

Introduction

Person: "Hey, how are you? Haven't seen you in ages?"

Me: ~~"I am a failure and I want to be alone. I hate myself, I'm such a disappointment."~~

Me: "Awesome, thanks! Yeah, been really busy lately…"

This was the dialogue I used to have with people in real life. I was too used to telling people I was fine, but I was slipping on a mask and fading away. The traumatic, hopeless feelings kicking in, I felt the pain exceeding the resources for coping.

We are not taught how to live through pain or conflict at school. But, in the midst of these challenging times, I started to write. If I didn't do that, I would not be here today. Anxiety and depression are like walking around in circles with a massive open wound that no one sees. Your ability to reach out for help is muted, as trauma often oppresses our reason for being. It can slowly kill us, unless we find inspiration again. People often fail to reach out to us when we are struggling and it's up to us to find our inspiration, even in our darkest days. Only then do we have the chance to be a greater person than we ever thought we could be.

I was being cyber bullied and too weak to fight back. Experiencing hate is very difficult to deal with, regardless of where it comes from. It always cuts deep. I didn't think I would make it past winter. Some days I couldn't walk out of the house. I became physically and emotionally sick. How many lost lives is it going to take for people to realise that the horrible things they say cause pain? Too many. Therefore, we need to express ourselves, regardless of how bad we feel. Get it out. Clear your mind. Ask yourself, what would you write if you were not afraid? Consider yourself in a state of constant learning when you start and your writing can go through different stages. Angry rants in your private journal can turn into captivating and unique short stories. Short stories can turn into exciting novels or screenplays. When alienation had slipped into my personal life, picking up a pen stopped the growing emptiness I felt and it truly saved my life. I am so thankful for the writing process, that I want everyone to try it as a therapeutic gift. Writing helps us to understand ourselves and the universe around us, and if you have been through a traumatic experience, it can give you that spark to take action in your own distinctive voice. This is the power of writing. It brings in the awareness, whether you decide to write from real life or imagination; a journal, a novel, a screenplay, a song, a poem, a short story... the choice is yours. Creative writing and self-management is also in demand as much as leadership and entrepreneur mindset in today's workplaces and having these skills will help you succeed.

It took me a long time to get back into any type of self-expression after being cyber bullied. I even struggled with social media posts and personal journals. Once I let go of the fear and felt the awareness of the writing, I started to live again. My unique voice had been buried underneath all that anxiety, post-traumatic stress disorder, panic attacks... you name it, for almost a decade, but it was not too late to get my voice heard once I made that decision. I did not suffer for nothing and I wasn't about to let all of that emotional pain lie undisturbed. The cyber bullies wanted me to simply disappear, but I thought about what I could write if I wasn't going to disappear and wasn't afraid anymore. I went ahead and did just that. Like most of us, I didn't want to retrieve painful memories, but it was the only way to survive and get over the stuck thoughts. Through writing I persisted with being positive again and stopped the vicious cycle of anxiety.

This book is for anyone who wants to use creativity as a tool after suffering any type of trauma and start the process of writing and creating. What makes people not even try writing is the belief that writing is hard, you need to be able to create attention-grabbing sentences and that you must be perfect.

People may also tell you that 'time heals all wounds.' However, when your emotional balance is off, it's not that simple. You need to think about what you could be doing during that time to help yourself.

Follow your curiosity to find ideas and if the trauma, medication or anxiety you have experienced have made you think you will never have any original ideas and thoughts, write about your trauma, write about your life and experiences, no matter how bad. You don't need to consider your potential readers, just write for yourself. This will get you started.

When you start writing about your life, you don't start from the point of knowing nothing at all. You already know it all, better than anyone else. And, when your writing is honest and raw, your story will bloom off the page and form in the reader's mind without looking for sympathy or changes in your narrative. My initial writing was about finding a will to live, craving happiness and a more beautiful life again after the storm; finding the calm within myself. There isn't anything that can prepare anyone for constant bullying and its consequences, no matter your age. Ending up a victim of bullying as an older teenager or adult should never be downplayed with the suggestion that 'you are old enough, deal with it.' Bullying happens everywhere, in our personal lives, school and at the office. We have to stop the bullied being treated like they are the problem, dismissals in favour of the bullies and problems being covered up because no one knows or wants to deal with it. I wasn't able to deal with it until I started responding with creative writing. Anyone who has ever been on medication for anxiety, post-traumatic stress disorder or depression knows that strategic thinking becomes hard, fantasising of anything at all is limited, your thought process is clouded and you start lacking original ideas. However, if you keep creating, you will get the hang of it again. You build resilience through creative response. Writing about your trauma can help you overcome it and journaling can distract you from your negative thoughts. Write about when you went for a run up those big hills and the weather was so hot. When you came back, you saw your bright red reflection in the mirror in the lift of your building. The neighbour smiled at you. What did you see when you went driving around in the city? Maybe you stopped as you saw an incident on the side of the road? Travel is one of my favourite things to write about. Reminiscing about the most beautiful areas on the coast, being captivated by small towns, great nights out and making wonderful friends.

You can write about how your travel kicked off, your arrival, what you did when you were there, how you felt when it was time to leave and any advice or recommendations you have for the reader. I have found that travel writing is one of the best ways to immerse myself fully in a different environment.

We all have times when we feel regret, but writing can help you to put mistakes and failures aside and aspire to live life without regrets. Writing will make you feel capable of pivoting and taking a new journey when it feels right; just like personal growth creates openings and closings.

Write stories of love, travel, culture and art. Memoirs of childhood, stories full of symbolism and mysteries, twists and turns. Write in first person, write in third person, share inspiration, knowledge and imagination. Realise that the time you spent feeling pain and sorrow was for this reason; to evolve through creative writing. The secret to success is to use the pain to get back in control of your life. Make use of all the setbacks instead of letting them get you down; it's all about trying a different approach.

I
UNLEASH YOUR CREATIVITY

My story

Sitting on a busy commuter train on the way to work, I was struggling to keep my eyes open. I had been awake all night with a severe, sharp pain shooting up my leg, but taking time off work was out of the question in the busy publishing office.

The sharp pain got worse and I was being referred from doctor to doctor. I attended physiotherapy that brought no relief. After having my daughter, the pain disappeared for a while, but my ankle remained swollen. I had moved across the world a few years earlier and had none of my own family around. My partner, who was in the military, was away occasionally for long periods of time. This was not an issue, but what came next in the midst of my new life overseas, no one could have prepared for. The bullies. They were looking for an outlet for their own anger and obsession with airing their views publicly online. They enlisted others to join in and used social media as a platform to amplify their attacks. My partner's military colleagues were quick to alert us when hateful posts appeared so that they could be deleted. The hate and anger coming from the bullies was shocking, considering they didn't know us from a bar of soap. They were publicly humiliating us, with their views that somehow we were less valuable people, being 'immigrants.' A military colleague of my partner's had a taste of it too; not only for defending us, but for being from another country originally. Social media makes it all the more possible for the cyber bullies to find out little details about our lives, and they are always looking for our weakest links to hit us with.

I had always had a passion for health and fitness, and, in addition to everything else, I decided to do a fitness instructor course. Towards the end of my course, the pain in my leg was back and my ankle swelled up even more. Despite the pain, I tried to carry on circuit training, dancing and weight training.

As I finished the course with flying colours, it all became physically impossible. I finally got a referral to an orthopaedic surgeon, who referred me for tests with a metabolic diseases specialist in another hospital. The specialist sat me down and explained that I was suffering from an incurable bone disease; pregnancy-induced AVN, or avascular necrosis, which literally means 'death of the bone.' AVN had been eating away at my right leg since I had become pregnant.

I was advised to talk to the orthopaedic surgeon again regarding what could be done for my leg. Another young mother attending the metabolic diseases specialist's clinic had pregnancy-related AVN in her hips and, at the age of 24, needed a hip replacement. It was likely my AVN would spread to other parts of my body, but for now, I was desperate to find out what could be done for my leg.

I was trying to remain positive and googled different medical alternatives, but having such a rare disease, it was hard to find information.

My anxiety reached a peak at the orthopaedic surgeon's office when he, without sugar-coating the news, told me that there may be a possibility my leg might have to be amputated below the knee at some point due to the necrosis. He had been corresponding with his colleagues around the world about alternative options and come to the conclusion that ankle fusion was the best option to hold the joints together and prevent the ankle collapsing for now. I agreed, but had to wait for the surgery. "What if I get it in my hips too?" I wondered as the radiating pain crept up my leg.

I single-handedly ran the household, dealing with the strains of military life, and to top it all, I was wearing a large boot to support my leg, trying to get around until I purchased a knee scooter to assist me. The chronic pain kept me up most nights until I had holes drilled in my bones and screws inserted.

My story

Waking up in the surgery after the operation and realising that I could never run or jump again, make use of my fitness course or even have full movement of my ankle was a small price to pay to keep my leg for now.

As I was recovering from the surgery, injecting myself daily with blood thinners, cyber bullying started again. Public humiliation, shared with people around the world who hadn't even known of our existence before.

Blocking and reporting doesn't stop cyber bullies, as I discovered. Friends still forwarded the worst posts for me to read, and I couldn't believe my eyes. They were ganging up, recruiting others and, worst of all, they were using the mean gas-lighting technique bullies often engage in.

When my partner posted a simple picture of a piece of jewellery he had bought me as a birthday present on social media, instant comments made my stomach turn; *"They should go back to where they came from," "Immigration is a hot topic"* and various other personal attacks. Needless to say, I never wore the jewellery and got rid of it.

The fact that I was not able to commute to work due to my worsening condition at that point was not left out either. One of the posts read: *"I actually have a job, unlike that specimen"* whilst in her profile pictures, the bully was, in fact, wearing clothes I had donated! Oh the irony of bullying! This could only be an indicator that, sadly, there was jealousy involved, which is often the cause of bullying. What kind of person wears a dress, coat and even wraps herself in a pink cotton scarf that had been warming the neck of the person they are bullying?

The universe is always trying to tell us something. And, it can be something simple. I should understand that, despite everything that happened to me, I still had the same big heart and broad understanding as I did when I was donating excess clothing without expectations. No matter who ends up wearing it, it won't change me or what I am about.

I found a photo of me cycling along the Golden Gate bridge in San Francisco, smiling and wearing that same pink scarf. Looking at the photo, my chronic, radiating pain got worse and I just collapsed on the couch. Dealing with bullies is hard in so many ways but you need to go back to your broader understanding. The most selfless act is to give without expectations, even to your enemies.

However, as the cyber bullying went on, I dosed up on anti-depressants to combat the feelings of worthlessness and loneliness brought on by it all. It wasn't the physical pain that was killing me, but the emotional.

One rainy Christmas, a friend invited my daughter and I to their house so that we wouldn't have to be alone. I hadn't been cleared to drive a car yet, but in desperation and sick of the loneliness, I took the car keys and, in the heavy rain, drove us to my friend's place.

The little drive around the city backfired and I was in extreme pain with my leg for the rest of the week, but at least I had a chance to socialise.

Eventually, the bullying and public humiliation hurt me to the extent that I perceived love as pain, and after going through therapy, I felt anger, not towards anyone else, but towards myself. I had been unable to walk away from it all with one leg, but I could have fought back. My therapist told me to stand up for myself and others, but I was too weak. She advised me that it was never too late to do something; bullies always find someone to target, someone they see as weak, to make themselves look more powerful. Nevertheless, all the hurtful words became my stuck thoughts.

My therapist read all the posts and emails, and repeatedly told me to stop being a victim and fight back; save and file everything. No one should be exposed to bullying, no matter the circumstances. And, the cyber bullying never stopped, not even when our circumstances changed. As my partner was posted with the military to a different state for training for a year, we lived separately, which is common within the military. This period only showed the reality of the situation, and all the public threats for us to leave the country, *"It's a game, we will win. They don't stand a chance,"* served no purpose, as nothing would have changed. Nevertheless, my partner made up a lie that he had, in fact, after all this, moved across the country to a very remote location.

It's been years and the bullies have no idea of the truth. My partner chose to lie in order to carry on with the mindful nonreaction towards the bullies, as years earlier he had written an open letter with print-outs of the emails and social media posts highlighting the abuse.

Sometimes the cold truth is that you cannot teach bullies to take responsibility for their actions, because for them, it's always easier to blame others for their behaviour, and psychological disengagement from the bullies is more important to the victim and others involved than attempting to make them understand. And, whereas most of us are unlikely to be able to psychologically disengage that way, I tried to understand that we are all different people with different ways of dealing with things. And, after all this, the same bullies are still most likely walking around wearing my donated clothing.

Having a background in media and communications, I decided to use this and sit down, put my boot up and write. It literally saved my life and pulled me out of the victim mentality, depression and anxiety. I ended up researching online bullying, writing articles about being bullied as an adult and even a full-length novel. As for my condition, I have now been diagnosed with AVN in both legs, am having more surgery and feeling chronic pain in my hips daily.

I felt the emotional torment with every cell of my body and compared to this, the physical challenges still felt minor. Nonetheless, everything that happened made me return to writing and this was the only way to defend my life and get the bullies out of my head space. I felt that I had stopped enjoying life and the stuck thoughts made me fail by default. Now, I will continue my fight against bullying. I know how fortunate I am to survive the emotional pain, as there are so many others not so lucky. My previous success, degrees, languages I had learned and the good people I had met and kept in my life suddenly meant nothing. I became very sick on top of my AVN. I dealt with a host of health issues and was diagnosed with post dramatic stress disorder (PDSD), anxiety, insomnia, severe migraines with daily aura and loss of vision nearly rupturing my brain, IBS, and on top of all that, my leg wasn't healing after the surgery. I had been living a life as a perpetual victim for almost a decade.

As I was writing, feeling anger and resentment, a miracle happened. I slowly started to thank the bullies. I felt gratitude for what they put me through.

I no longer care about the horrible things they say and write on social media, which they still continue to do; even turning on each other. I feel more inspired and positive about life than ever, and instead of fearing the worst for my legs, I imagine myself on my feet again, my beautiful daughter by my side.

Through writing, I have been able to identify what I really want, and more importantly, why. I was writing my way out. When you realise why you want something in life, you gain motivation and energy to achieve it all. For me, it was the realisation that I had overcome everything that was meant to destroy me. I felt the need to write, even though the writing process is not easy; sometimes you feel like you're taking two steps forward and one back all the time. I had to keep going, because thousands of people out there are being bullied, publicly humiliated or traumatised, trying to come to terms with past or present suffering. Life would be easy if we could all use kindness as a tool for transformation, but anyone who has been through challenging times knows it's just not enough; there is always darkness involved. When writing my first novel, I went through both hellfire and holy water, through characters entering darkness and light. Without even thinking about it at the time, through creative writing, I was creating meaning and understanding for my own life. As corny as it sounds, the bullies thought they were breaking me, but in reality they were making me. The writing process put everything in perspective for me, the bullies started to feel distant and slowly I felt I was back in control of my life. I no longer wasted any energy or thought on hating them, and that in itself was a success. The entire process of writing that first novel was more important than the outcome of it. I didn't care if it got published or not, as I was already an award-winning novelist of my own life.

The reason why I held back for so long with writing was the need for perfection, but you don't need to be perfect to inspire others. Let people feel inspired by how you deal with your imperfection, as none of us are perfect. Never be ashamed of your story, as it might inspire others.

I kept quiet for a decade about the abuse, because I felt powerless and scared. I also tried too hard to tap into the compassion that I had been taught to show all through my childhood. I kept defending the bullies and why they did this to me, thinking fear makes people do bad things and that people like them, who wake up in the morning with a decision to harm others, have been pushed to the limits somehow; that something triggered the bullying. I have been taught to forgive and turn the other cheek, and I did all this for a decade. It made me mistrust myself and during that time I wrote notes like the one below. Throughout this book, I will show you how my mindset has transformed through creative writing; from the text below to something much more inspiring.

"I pray for the God who does not answer.

I place a shrine of incense, crystals and flowers. I wait… for a resolution that never comes, unanswered questions, lingering in the air behind the grey clouds.

The reality of life is nothing but pain and sorrow, a black cloud of fear rolling all over you. You will never overcome it, because no one is there for you."

This shows how bullying causes us to hide behind a veil and fail by default. It leaves deep scars and recovery is a difficult, depressing, dark, long road. In the aftermath, whilst we are trying to protect ourselves, we also stop living.

It slowly blurs and distorts our vision and perception of ourselves; the discomforting confusion we have to wade through just prior to experiencing clarity. Bullying causes psychological uncertainty even in the most confident people and this is what my story is about. I'm hoping that coping mechanisms, overcoming fears with strategies, building self-esteem and becoming more assertive will help you to defend your life. The truth is, we may never find that final closure, and the question is, do we even need to? Your life is an art, and no matter how painful your experience, it will make you stronger once you let it create something meaningful.

The secret of building reliance lies in your daily thoughts and routines, and accepting things as they are doesn't mean you need to hide behind your veil for the rest of your life. Life is never perfect and plans rarely work out as we want them to. We mature with the damage, not with the years; but if you turn the damage into wisdom, you are back in control of your life.

I am hoping this book will guide you through the state of transition into creative writing and to the higher ground of living your life the way you deserve to.

I started to see myself in the spotlight with amazing clarity, leaving behind the veil the bullies threw over me. I tried a lot of other ways to recover. Writing gave me an opportunity to turn my wounds into wisdom, and that was my road to recovery.

There are lot of negative, bad people in this world. When you have had the misfortune of experiencing them in your life one way or another, it's easy to get so enraged that you resort to something that gives you instant gratification and seeming success; it's the voice in your head inviting you to the dark side. You start acting with bad intentions, and it can drag you into its depths and feel satisfying, momentarily. I ended up in darkness for years, and it sparked me to write a sinister story about an immigrant woman who orders a New Orleans voodoo doll online and, step by step, gets dragged into the dark, spiritual world of black magic. To feel the dark side of spirituality, I ordered a voodoo doll from New Orleans in real life. It was beautiful, with golden clothes and a black face with big, white, oval eyes staring right back at me. I became fascinated by this doll, knowing it was a medium to my message in the dark story. The pins I pushed into its cushioned body were not enough for my character. I took the doll to the graveyard with me and started to dig the soil, feeling the character's pain in understanding how it feels to not be truly free. At that time, I was still being cyber bullied, and as crazy as it may sound, writing about my character's intentions to pay back through black magic and the trips to the graveyard to feel connected to the story helped me to gain control and let go of my own trauma.

When we go through any trauma, especially bullying, our survival mechanisms are constantly heightened and our brains are tuned in to potential threats. In the long term, we become addicted to the idea of being a victim who believes there is nothing we can control. We give up the constant battle to achieve success and start to concentrate on protecting ourselves instead, leading to unhappiness.

This is exactly what happened to me.

Why write? Finding your way to inspired writing

Emotional pain, for me, felt like severe chest pain, confusion, utter sadness and hopelessness, and I felt like this for a decade. During this time, I questioned why me, every single day. I had no choice but to start thinking there is a purpose on this; the severe pain I felt was a signal for something larger than this. I had to start using the bullies to my own advantage and learn from the unpleasant life experience they had thrown at me. They made me feel the pain. And the pain made me think more sharply.

There is always something you can gain from bullies. They have picked you as a target, so you must be something unique already, if people are jealous of and feel anger towards you. The fact that I was different, successful and from an unfamiliar culture, as well as their own fear made them shout racist remarks at me. Once I got rid of the stuck thoughts by writing them down, I was able to recognise my value and worth as an immigrant. A proud immigrant, not one that was suffering. The truth is that bullies can't empathise with those who are suffering, therefore they think it is all a game, and if they ever see your pain, they think they have won. It stimulates them; serves a purpose in justifying and adding value to their delusional lives. Nevertheless, whilst their lives were consumed by gaining value by abusing others, I started to use their abuse as a tool. When they wrote online, *"Go back to where you came from, immigrant,"* I actually did, but through meditation and writing. I gained spiritual strength by doing so, and with that strength I broke free from victim mode. Having a new daily habit to break free from abuse is crucial.

I closed my eyes and imagined being a small child back in the 1980s. It was a cold January night; the temperature had dropped to the minus 30s. I was wearing my red felt fabric winter boots. Every little step I took, the snow under the boots whispered to me with its crisp voice. I felt calm and happy. I looked up and saw countless stars and a bright moon; the cold air making my nose tingle. I felt so contented. I returned to that moment in my mind whenever I started to feel agitated. I instantly felt calm again and my heart stopped racing. And that is why I am thankful to the bullies for trying to publicly humiliate me by writing on social media *"Go back where you came from."* Without that specific insult, I would not have recovered that beautiful memory among thousands of others, which made me calm and happy again.

I also wrote other short stories about childhood memories, which helped speed up my recovery. We all have stories to tell, and picking up a pen and letting it all flow can be liberating. I didn't have a plan for what I was going to write, but I ended up writing a full-length novel; a fish out of water story about an immigrant girl desperately trying to use the supernatural to get herself and others out of a dangerous and bad situation. The lesson in the novel is that we are all meant to grow so that we have something to give. I wish I could have written something different, something about joy, happiness and contentment, because at times, when I was writing, the worry and the fear came back, and I brought more of it into my life rather than release it. It had to be done, it had to be written. I compare it to walking in a forest and screaming at the top of your lungs.

Sitting in the cold library basement, I didn't stop to reflect on my writing, I just kept going. In my solitude, my thoughts and feelings of anger, depression and resentment kept coming out, page by page. Through writing, I was channelling the pain, and found that, I was often writing about snakes. Snakes represent creative life force, transformation and healing.

I was looking at the pain and rotating it, finding my own safe place to start healing. It can be anywhere you are able to think, write, meditate, dance or just breathe. I couldn't escape too far to find my safe place, but I felt secure and content in the local library, among all the unknown people working on their projects or reading. I found myself in the basement of this beautiful building with my flask of coffee, five days a week, for one entire year. I took my lunch with me, a can of tuna and a piece of fruit, and sat outside in the courtyard to eat it, whilst looking at the garden and the ocean. My painfully agitated mind was forced into this beautiful, tranquil environment and I had no choice but to fight the feelings of anger and hate; the world outside was too beautiful for it.

Once I was back in the basement, I poured the creativity out. Daily habits like this force you to make the shift into healing. The single force that changed everything for me was my decision to go to the library basement on a daily basis. I wasn't able to control events, but I could control my choices.

I committed to growing out of the pain by writing almost every day. The stuck thoughts, such as, "I'm being bullied, I'm being put down" needed to go away. Bullying, or any trauma, is an intense experience; your destiny depends on your commitment to race out of it. Writing may seem like a slow way to get out, but it's still one of the best ways, as well as reading and studying.

Sometimes I stopped writing and studied things like Buddhism. One story stuck in my mind. It compared suffering and emotional pain to being hit by two arrows; we have no control over the first arrow that hits us (consider this the bullies), but the second arrow is shot by ourselves. What this means is that we can't stop the bullies hurting us, but we can do a lot to halt the second arrow; we can focus on our own reactions and, from my experience, this is often all we can do.

When the first wave of emotions subsided, I started to look at the situation not only through the creative side, but also through the eyes of the corporate business communicator I used to be. I reminded myself that the cruel remarks were the bullies' opinions, not facts, and chose to seek out and concentrate on things that were factual, not the interpretations or emotional reactions of other people. I also reminded myself that to get through the emotional pain, I must learn to tolerate discomfort and vulnerability.

The creative writing allowed me to step away from being the victim of bullying; with the pen in my hand, I was in control. I placed my anger and resentment onto the paper and even though it was still consuming almost every thought, at least it was coming from a place of empowerment and I was letting it all out.

Fear of shedding the mask

I remember when the raging elephant in the room told me it's time to shed the mask and be who I am or exit the stage and never come back. The little rebel started yelling underneath my skin for me to grab a pen, and like a pressure cooker, I was busting for release. I've never felt more real. And then the fear crept in, the subconscious reaction. Fear changes our perceptions. Imagine walking on the wharf in sunny Florida. A wild dolphin splashes in the glistening water, waiting for leftover fish from the local fisherman. One of the fishermen smiles at you and asks if you would like to feed the dolphin. "Feed the dolphin?" you ask cautiously, because someone told you scary stories about wild dolphins being as deadly as alligators, costing you an arm and a leg. You feel doubtful, but the fisherman's confident smile convinces you otherwise. You kneel down nervously, and the dolphin snaps the fish from your hand. As the dolphin swims away, you feel amazing and forget all about your fears, because your perception has changed.

One night I couldn't sleep, because I suddenly remembered a mother from school complaining about the traffic fine she had received when dropping her daughter off. This story planted in my mind. I started panicking that I had performed similar traffic violation when dropping my child off. Now that I had this fear in my mind about the possible fine, big enough to cause me financial difficulties, I started to panic. The fear crept up on me and I imagined the worst outcome. Maybe I was sent the fine a long time ago but never received it, as some of our post had gone missing. The fine would be tripled by now! The issue grew bigger and bigger in my head until there was no way I could peacefully go to sleep.

I jumped online and started looking around to see if there was any way I could check on this. No, I had to wait until the morning and call the revenue office then. Of course, I ended up with a sleepless night.

In the morning, I was making my coffee and waiting impatiently on hold for the revenue, my heart pounding, thinking, "How can I afford this?" and "What if my daughter can't go on the school camping trip now?" These thoughts raced through my head as I rambled my registration number and the lady at the other end of the line said, "No. No fines."

I felt relieved, but I also hated myself for letting the anxiety take control and ruin my sleep over absolutely nothing! Whereas fear is a subconscious reaction, remaining calm is a trained response. Most of the things we are fearful about we have projected onto ourselves through our perceptions. If we use our imaginations and find our inner storyteller instead, we start seeing things with our mind's eye. Imagination, like perception, lets us see things that aren't necessarily true, but also gives us a creative attitude. With creative attitude, you can let go of stuck thoughts.

My anxiety started breeding chaos in my life and the post-traumatic stress disorder, born out of emotional trauma, made every single abusive word from a bully's mouth grow bigger and bigger in my head, until I completely lost my self-confidence. I even stopped sharing great things on social media because the perception I had of my abilities and personal worth had been crushed by the bullies.

Can you imagine going travelling to somewhere truly amazing and not telling anyone?

Can you imagine seeing magical places and meeting amazing people and telling no one?

How would that make things? Better or worse?

My therapist told me to start sharing again on social media, despite knowing that the bullies were spying on me. "Intelligent people ignore," she said. "Let them see you."

I wasn't capable of doing this, because the fear took over everything. I reflected on the problem and all the suffering I was carrying around; the baggage of fear and resentment. It put an obstacle in my path. Social media is nothing but a snapshot of real life. It is not a reflection of it, so why did I care?

I needed my self-belief back to neutralise all that fear within me. It was constantly sabotaging all my efforts; even the smallest attempts to write and communicate again.

I have been teaching others how to communicate. I have studied and learned how leaders communicate, how to converse with large groups, small groups, individuals, but never, ever, did I stop and think about how I communicate with myself. How we communicate with ourselves is integral to our success.

The turning point, again, was the role of victim I had assumed after being bullied. I was always making the point in business communication that it is important to use appropriate words and have the right mindset. In my personal life, I was not doing as I was preaching. I used words such as, "If the bullies ever leave me alone" or "If it ever ends," instead of adopting the mindset that it is going to pass and will all be over, and saying *"When* the bullies leave me alone" and *"When* the bullying ends." With stuck thoughts, there was no "when."

I thought about my business background and how we spoke to employees and clients. We didn't use fear-mongering. I decided to try this strategy and talk to myself the same way, for one whole day. I started by using positive and happy stories from my past. Instead of projecting fearful stories into my mind, I pulled a box of old photographs down and only picked the ones where I looked the happiest I had ever been. I reminisced about the uplifting stories behind the photos. This led me to remember other stories from my past that illustrated the point that I was once a happy and successful person.

I asked myself questions. What was it that made me happy at that point in life? How did I achieve that success? Would I do anything differently if I could?

By questioning and listening to myself, I adopted the role of the receiver. You are all those things; you are your past successes and you are that happy person. Something just got lost along the way. Why do people have their favourite bible quotes and books, radio and television shows, movies and songs? People like repetition, consistency and simplicity, and this is exactly how successful communication works. This is also how you need to start communicating with yourself, to get over things and people. Go back to basics and start using the words "when" instead of "if" and you will get there. I used writing to get to know myself better and to feel more comfortable with who I am. Finding the unique YOU before starting to write will help you to shed the fear. Set yourself a set of resourceful questions and seek for answers that help you achieve what you want. The fear is just a belief that something is holding you back. Release the false illusion of fear that stops you from taking action. It's pointless having concepts and plans if you are too fearful to take action. You need to snap out of the fear cycle and redeem yourself in public, in the presence of your bullies. Once this is done, the fear is gone.

Awareness of communication – what do writing and creative expression offer?

Everyone has a creative streak. We often find this streak deep inside us after realising that life is not simple; it is not black and white. Let creativity bring some colour to your life, because you don't become the person you are without experiencing both the good and the bad. The power and confidence to express ourselves hides behind fear, but what are we afraid of, exactly? There is nothing to be afraid of, nothing to stop our creativity, so let it flow. A strong mind can help you through anything. In a way it is the strongest 'muscle' in our body and if you are not using it, you are losing your power. Harnessing it for creative work will not only give you your power back, it will also free you from the stuck thoughts. It can also help you to begin the healing process, by acknowledging the trauma you may have experienced. The negative things did happen to you, but you were not responsible for them. And, by keeping your mind strong by writing it all out, you can get past obstacles in life.

Your creative work doesn't need to be perfect. You can let other people be inspired by your imperfections, as no one is perfect. This will allow you to find confidence and uniqueness, which will ultimately lead to your new-found happiness and success in life. The notion that your writing has the power to shape someone's life should spark thousands of thoughts, of which one or two will turn into a creative piece that makes a worthy point.

Writing can feel like moving towards light from the darkness. We see all the art forms, inside or outside, like three-dimensional drawings. We analyse our work, often looking for imperfections when we could just simply be 'imperfectly perfect' for our readers.

Writing can be as simple as taking the things you know and rearranging them into a storyline. And that's when we open new doors to magic moments.

When your fears take a toll on your creativity, you can't force yourself to become self- expressive. I have lost the flow of my inspiration, felt stuck and misplaced with my work. During those times, it is essential not to lose hope, but take a small break, listen to music, go for a walk and discover something new. Inspiration is always around us, but we can go blind to it all momentarily, as if our curiosity needs a break. If we seek to write about deeper meanings in our stories, we need to consider the matter of focus, and without motivation, we can't focus. I wanted to write a second part to my novel, but completely lost all motivation. I couldn't even think of an idea to start with, let alone focus. I was doing my daily routine tasks, school runs, cleaning, washing, going to the supermarket... then it slowly occurred to me; I had been writing before because the emotional pain was killing me and I needed to let it out. I had a spark and a reason to write. I wanted to survive mentally, and without the writing process, I would not have. I hadn't lost my spark for writing, I had finally got over the worst pain. I did not need to write about pain and suffering, abuse and betrayals to feel better anymore. I could write about happy and enjoyable things now. I had grown as a writer and it was time to move onto a new field of themes. I felt inspired to explore different types of writing. When you are not too hard on yourself, you can discover natural affinity with writing, a door to growth. Consider writing as good art that makes you feel powerful and adventurous by treating your story like a conversation with a unique point of view. The reason I wanted to write about bullying was because I was tired of hateful behaviour; the vicious cycle of it going on in real life and online. I wanted action and to shift the focus. You click on the other world that exists online to escape, only to face a negative environment worse than the real world. The online world should be safe, happy and encouraging, not emotionally painful and humiliating. If you have been a victim of bullying in any shape or form, you know that we want action not sympathy. And, if you can find something creative to occupy your time with and love what you do, it is not only easier to get over things, but you will care less about the things that happen online. Also, it will help you to resist the urge to delay your happiness until some point in the future and discover your hidden talents. Hidden talents are like natural resources, buried beneath. We do not know what lies inside us until we try different things.

I tried really hard to learn piano, coming from a somewhat musical family. I mastered the basics, but I never fully enjoyed playing. I closed the piano lid at the age of twelve and haven't played since. Playing piano wasn't my thing and didn't change my quality of life like another creative form did; writing.

A consequence of bullying and abuse can be that you see your life as they set it out for you; miserable and pointless. For me, it took one year to shift the focus from negative feelings, fear and depression. And that one year was spent in the library basement writing and working on my mindset. By refusing to tolerate any kind of bullying, online or real life, we can change our mindset from seeking sympathy to seek action.

This is how I shifted the focus and changed the story when bullies wrote *"Immigrant bitch"* in a hateful and negative manner on a public domain:

An immigrant is someone who has travelled, taken a huge, bold step into the unknown and created a life on another continent. Part of being truly alive is ending up on a 'quest' or journey. Life is not linear. Life is an organic quest. I opened myself up to the world around me and in their eyes, I failed the quest in every single part of my life; where I was living, my career, my personal life. They summarised that I was a total failure. I was judged by their fear of me; they did not know me in real life. Whatever bullies think should not matter.

When we judge other people, it can be dangerous. Wisdom is replaced by so-called knowledge from social media; we no longer relate to the world at large. Bullies have a very narrow focus that does not encapsulate the whole picture. Turn to people who are trying to create an encouraging, safe and positive place for everyone, either online or in real life, because bullies are only trying to shift your focus and make you believe that you have failed when you have not. Our world can collapse in one second; the tables can turn any day. I know how to deal with trauma and sorrow because bullies put me through it. Do the bullies have this ability? Remember, you are stronger than them because they turned you into a resilient, successful person and writing can enrich the lives of people who have been lead to believe they have failed. You never failed. They did, because nothing good can ever come of being hateful.

I reached the top of my education and career once before, but I didn't feel it was what I wanted and, at 24, I experienced burn-out. One morning, I collapsed on a busy London bus on the way to work. All I remember is being carried off the bus by friendly American tourists who gave me bread and water. The pressure was on; I couldn't see inside myself. I hadn't been letting my intuition flow. I collapsed, physically and mentally. Instead of gaining the experience and knowledge to be able to take a whole new approach, I just kept going with the same. I got another job in the media and put myself in an even trickier situation. I wasn't capable of the role. I shone in the interview and beat hundreds of other applicants, but I didn't listen to myself, even after burning out. I thought I could go on, even in a position that required high-level analytical skills, which I found out I didn't exactly possess, being more of a creative soul.

The role was in a television station and they put their trust in me, on a Friday, to schedule the weekend programmes. I didn't count the gaps correctly and the channel went black for a while one Sunday. They still believed in me, and instead of sacking me, they gave me a private maths lesson! This is proof that no matter what, there are always people in this world who believe in you. They are not necessarily your family or friends, but people who see your potential. I went full-steam ahead without hearing that little voice within, giving me the right direction.

Intuition can be a valuable communication tool that reflects your own energy. I was trying to figure out why I was lacking in certain areas. Was it because I didn't believe enough, or something else? Knowing that I hadn't been paying attention to my intuition, I adopted a creative attitude. My mind's eye saw colours, shapes, characters and scenarios. Imagination helped me overcome my lack of intuition and I found my inner storyteller.

If you want to inspire others with your writing, go back and think of all the challenges and things you used to struggle with in your childhood and adolescence. You were served these challenges for a reason and you overcame everything.

If you're looking for writing inspiration, you could go walking across a river. You may have to step on rocks to avoid falling in the water, and it may be challenging, but it brings you back to basics; how you feel and experience the world around you.

Sometimes I reminisce about walking in the snow. How magical it felt, the sounds it made, the texture, the coldness. In my imagination, I walk into a forest as clouds continue to roll on by. In the distance, the trees whisper to me, seeking my company again. I smile, realising how lucky I am to feel nature's calming presence. I'm in a relationship with the world itself again, and I write about the waves, the clouds and the stars on my journey. I didn't listen to intuition, but that is part of the quest called 'Life.' Write about the world around you; when you notice the night's first star as the sky turns darker or when you walk on the beach and the ocean speaks to you. Write about feeling the wind blow, or imagine you *are* the wind. Or when you are in a city amongst thousands of people but feel alone. The world around you can be a building block for your writing.

Awareness of communication is the sense of knowledge from within. When you embrace painful trauma as part of your foundation through writing, you see beauty in where you are now; you survived. Our world is a functional one. The skill of understanding what other people are feeling is vanishing, especially with cyber bullying, trolling and public humiliation online.

Going into the unknown is number one for living your life. When you go on a journey, you face a big chance of failure. We need to be ready to fail, because failure is part of the journey. And, as the bullies saw me as a complete failure, I knew I had, in fact, succeeded.

Everything they were saying was just noise from an external world. I had to rewire my brain to tune out that noise and disconnect myself. If life keeps throwing you negative experiences like it did for me, find the imagination from inside yourself and change the story. Take a break from the negative environment, in real life and online.

You can't avoid the opinions of others, or hurtful words, but you can turn them into a library and use them as resources. Start creating you. Construct yourself again by picking up a pen, because within you there is valuable wisdom and insight. There comes a point in life where, in order to succeed, you must do the thing you think you can't do; shift the focus and change the story, just like I did when I was called 'immigrant bitch.' When I was called more names, like *"jobless loser immigrant"* and told to *"Go back to where you came from,"* I changed the story to; *"Go back to your roots."* I looked into my own background and history; even going as far as my country's mythology, which is very interesting. Once again, thank you bullies!

The turning point was also understanding my own behaviour. I had turned into a passive-aggressive person, giving other people silent treatments and disappearing. My confidence had taken such a huge hit, that if I had even a minor disagreement or something didn't go as planned, in my mind it was better for everyone if I vanished from the picture. I could drop out of contact for weeks or months. It was my way of protecting myself. I constantly felt uncomfortable. And I realised I had some toxic traits myself. When I felt uncomfortable, I was the one hurting people around me until I admitted that I let the toxic cycle continue because I was hurting. This vicious cycle needs to be shut down, knowing that anyone who has ever said "sticks and stones can break my bones but words will never hurt me" has never been verbally bullied in their life. Internet trolls don't have the understanding that someone out there is, or could be, upset, but the pleasure they get out of abuse is only temporary. If you help people and make them feel better, some of that happiness stays with you and is a far more permanent joy than the bullies and trolls get. You cannot fix hateful people by making laws that prevent hurtful speech. The best way to ensure our freedom of speech is to ignore the bullies and trolls. Emotional pain eats away at your mental strength and unhealthy beliefs about yourself and self-pity keep you focused on the problem.

There is a time in your life when you need all your mental strength. It is like physical strength; you need to adopt good habits and give up bad ones. Feeling sad, angry and hurt; I went through these pains feeling like my chest was exploding. We have to go through the discomfort to get to the comfort.

After a while, I felt exhausted and my head was hurting, but the strong, emotional pain shattering my chest had slowly gone. It made me think; how was it even possible for someone who had already been through so much to become a whinging victim of the bullies?

The challenging road kicked off in my childhood. I had to survive extreme weather conditions of minus 30 degrees! When I was living in these conditions, I never realised how strong I was mentally. The muscles of my legs felt like ice when I walked and my eyelashes turned into tiny ice sticks. I didn't have to train to adapt to the tough environment around me. With the bullies, this was the key; adaptation. How had I let them make me feel so overwhelmed when I was able to fly through harsh physical conditions without letting it stop me? The answer lies in my mindset and fear. I was never fearful of the unforgiving conditions, because I was born in this environment. I was confident I wasn't going to freeze to death.

Survivors are those who can overcome the greatest obstacle of them all: the mind. When you feel like giving up, remember, we want the world to be fair, but you have to accept that it isn't. My unhealthy habits were holding me back and I realised that the easiest way to get my self-confidence back was to do what I was most scared of, no matter the odds. What I didn't acknowledge (and if I had, I would have been more resilient) is that it takes a lot of courage to show your dreams to someone else. Here I was, writing, regardless of whether it was fiction or non-fiction, holding my heart out to the entire world. It can't get any braver than that. From that library basement, I slowly started to build resilience through creative writing. I was slowly bouncing back, by exposing the pain, despite my vulnerability. The writing was turning my pain into power, all my fears into focus and the difficulties I was facing into blessings. The shift was happening.

I watched my daughter playing with a kaleidoscope and I looked at the structure of it. It's filled with broken bits and pieces, but looking through all these broken bits, you see something beautiful, and this is what life is like for most of us. The resilience comes from tapping into your uniqueness; that's when your value shines.

In my case, at first I was fearful that by going public with my writing, I would do what everyone says not to do when dealing with bullies; I would let everyone know that their hurtful words got to me and how they affected the lives of my family. I had had enough of remaining quiet about that horrible decade, and by being quiet, I was allowing them to carry it on for so long, encouraged to repeat and intensify their aggressive behaviour, towards other people too. Transformational writing gave me the power to rise above it. The helplessness, fear, shame and embarrassment were diminishing. Sharing my experience will strengthen my own ability to handle difficult situations and protect my right to create my own happy and healthy life; no more being threatened, mentally and emotionally.

The bullies always pick unique personalities; someone that somehow threatens them. However, they don't like challenge, as they are, deep down, the weak ones. Whilst you are working on your perseverance and resilience, building a wiser and stronger version of yourself, they are throwing their empty anger and hate around and getting nowhere. We are facing an epidemic in cyber bullying and this is where I found deeper meaning in what happened to me, too. There are millions of people who log on to the internet feeling a pit of anxiety in their stomach for what appears to be no reason. In reality, they are alarmed because of the trauma and fear of cyber bullying.

This is where we need to reframe our thinking and build resilience for these feelings. Everyone has a right to log on to the internet and social networking sites without fear and feelings of anxiety. Creativity is the most important human resource to overcome these feelings and progress. Creativity makes us focus on what's holding us together rather than what is tearing us apart, and with that direction, we survive.

Unleash successful content

Once I started writing, everything came pouring out of me with such force, I ended up with a very complex storyline in my first manuscript. Not only was it a fish out of water story, but it read like a soap opera, with complex international characters and themes.

I put all my excitement and passion into the story and was struck with the lightning power of commitment to finish a 90,000-word manuscript. However, after completion of the manuscript came disappointment and frustration. The manuscript read like a complete, complex mess. Although I had a lot of content, it was not directed at anyone specific. I could have accomplished something more significant with the powerful determination I had going on if I had stopped and asked the right questions before starting the process:

1) What will the reader get from reading my novel and what is the attention-grabber?

2) How do I keep them engaged until the end, with interesting and valuable content?

3) What is the 'call to action' after they've read it?

At the time, it was vital for me to let the writing flow without these questions, because the pain was empowering me. Although it would have been a lot easier if I had thought of these three things prior to writing, there is always the chance to go back and re-write with a fresh set of eyes. Small improvements strengthen your foundation of writing and eventually move you in the direction you desire. This also gives you an opportunity to build a strong, unique identity, far away from the victim that initially wrote thousands of words out of pain. You create value for yourself and your readers will listen to you.

The healing starts the day you begin to write; if you are trying to find meaning through it. We don't seek painful experiences, but we can endure great pain if it's purposeful.

When I first started writing at primary school, I wrote an essay for the Russian-Finnish friendship organisation, who, at that time, were busy building peaceful relations after the war. As I grew up, I listened to my grandfather, a war veteran, tell his stories and I understood that, in my culture, the cornerstone of our identity is to give pride to our country. By then, I had enough knowledge to write that war had left a melancholy void for both parties, yet war is about forging meaning and building identity. War puts things into perspective. The controversy still is the notion of war as a purposeful pain. In regards to bullying, if you hold on to the notion that the worst times makes us who we are, as with war, we can get past the hurtful comments and public humiliation. Everything stays online, especially on social media. Anyone who has ever tried to have someone else's post removed will know how hard it is. However, you can use this for your own benefit; as a creative source, no matter how painful. Thousands of war novels and movies are based on pain. Traumatic human experiences serve as creative sources. As I learned from my war veteran grandfather, breaking the silence will heal your pain. He spoke about the war and I wrote about it.

Creative writing is one of the best ways to live through our trapped emotions and develop awareness. We can use this awareness to realise that our gift is our story. When we have been through a painful period, we often become overthinkers. Without realising, we grow wiser than we thought possible.

Writing brings out the vulnerability in us, but also the emotional intelligence. The more we write, the more intelligent we get; using our personal energy, we achieve a higher frequency. Habits of successful writers often include understanding the power of reading, time management and routine, starting with small, monthly goals, which will eventually lead to bigger, more specific goals. Short creative writing exercising on a routine basis can lead to a full manuscript later on. Don't attempt to write a full-length manuscript at first go; start with short stories. Keep your content simple by using uncomplicated vocabularity instead of trying to sound clever with fancy words. Simplicity is the key.

The feeling of vulnerability and sharing your writing

Once you have enough written material, whether short stories, poems, novels or screenplays, you are halfway there, because half of the sense of wellbeing is in the writing. The other half comes from sharing your writing, which is a scary thought for writers overcoming vulnerability. There are others who can relate to and acknowledge your pain, and once you realise this, it will make you comfortable with your vulnerability, and the feeling of being heard gives you the power to help others and hopefully write more. The process is always more important than the outcome, and part of that process involves gaining back your sense of wellbeing and confidence. We are not only expressing something, but also building a reality. We can create a narrative with negative and dismissive content, but that doesn't encourage a positive and hopeful world. If we create one, even just *one* positive, balmy and indulgent dialogue, it can create an experience of inspiration for the reader. As with life, writing is not just about what you can get from it, but also what you can give to others. Helping others through writing gives the writer meaning.

This is a sentence I wrote about my grandmother. She passed away in hospital, with severe dementia, whilst I was on the other side of the world. I was unable to grieve, but able to write:

"She had eyes that saw things too far and her thoughts wandered off on voyages so far, but her presence was like a beam of light from the full moon..."

When you write and explore different types of writing, you learn the entire process of becoming a powerful, confident writer; discovering that meaningful bridge between the past and the present. As you can see, I brought shattered aspects of my experience of the death of my grandmother to my writing; using the past tense, but also showing hope.

There are plenty of people who have tried writing as therapy and don't find it emotionally helpful. Engaging in one type of writing, building on dismissive and negative characters without hope, cannot lead to a positive experience. To turn this around and not let it become an emotionally harmful experience, as we are not as self-aware as we think we are, we can look at writing a happy song, poem or just a few positive sentences. Writing in the moment and in retrospect, we often write made-up stories to tell the truths we deep down wish we could say out loud. Remember who you are, be proud of who you are, learn to value yourself again and engage in other activities of self-care as well as writing. Bring all of this together to focus on the qualities you most like about yourself.

As a post-traumatic stress disorder sufferer, I often feel overwhelmed with my writing and feel the emotional harm more than the good, but this is a passing feeling, because I know, deep down, that in the end, there is a purpose for my pain. To be able to express myself in writing in a way I can't in conversation and to give shape to images and link them to thoughts means that, one day, the right reader will be able to adapt the world I doubted and thought was naive and idealistic. Suddenly the story comes alive for someone else, when the consequence of your writing happens naturally. It delivers. It is up to you to make a creative space without judgement, fear or unnecessary drama.

I eventually got over the cyber bullying and realised it is up to me to create a social media space with limits, because there is so much 'noise' and a word out of place on social media can instantly create drama. If and when you go public with your writing, you should set these limits and only share the space with conscious readers. Negative energy, especially online, serves no purpose other than to limit potential for all. The process of writing is more important than the outcome and perfection in writing doesn't exist. Writers would never publish anything if they always aimed for perfection.

Let the writing follow its own course, and notice the change to an upgraded mindset, which leads to upgraded actions. Eventually, we start to call the shots again. No more being humiliated, bullied or traumatised. Writing gives us an opportunity and options. We have a choice. The flow of stories, songs and poems is constantly circling around you. Writing can be contagious and powerful; the smallest story shared can shift a whole energetic playing field somewhere. No one can tell us what to write, when to write and how to write; unless you are writing screenplays, but even these rules can be broken. Dare to be different! Film director Mika Kaurismaki made a feature-length movie entirely without a formal screenplay.

When you are sitting in a restaurant, take a look around you; the people, the food, the ambience. In one room already there are more stories than your pen can handle. You're not like everyone else, you are not average, and you are definitely not what the bullies say you are. Through writing you can challenge your limited-thinking patterns and know you are destined for greatness. The reason I started to write again was knowing that somewhere out there was someone counting on me to show up for them. Their life wouldn't be the same without me; they would be depressed, uninspired and humiliated. The secret of all of this is that you never know who is going to read your words and absorb it into their minds like smoke, reforming into its new environment. Your writing fulfills its purpose when your vision blooms off the page for the right reader. This was the thought that kept me going and forced me to focus on the positives in life after all the trauma, and realise that it is actually beautiful and the bad things can stay as a distant illusion; the daily feelings of failure, feeling lost and scared. I battled and persevered because life will always knock you down, you just need to find a way to stand up again. For me, that was through writing.

It took a long time for me to change the world around me and become more resilient. When you are being bullied, it is one of the loneliest times of your life. Especially when you're an adult; you don't want to admit that you are being hurt this way at your age. You feel embarrassment and shame that you somehow brought this on yourself and people will ask "What did you do to deserve this?" You are fearful that your life will be painted by isolated incidents and public humiliation. The bullies have intimidated you; mentally and emotionally undermined you.

Bullying hurts, no matter your age. Bullying prevents you from doing things the way you should. So how did I really get through all this just by picking up a pen and reclaiming my authentic self again? Inner power through self-knowledge, which leads to courage, recognising and working with my fears, using my anger as fuel and eventually realising that I could use my experience to my own benefit, to be a stronger person and help spread positive messages.

As much as I used to like writing about putting pins through voodoo dolls, snakes and curses in my first novel, I believe that we don't need to punish bullies; they need to be treated. I wrote such extreme scenarios as part of my own healing.

Dealing with real life bullies is problematic, as most refuse to recognise that they have ever done anything wrong. They will go on living their lives in exactly the same way, hurting others. Through writing, we should not only reach out to help ourselves, but maybe one day, the bullies and abusers themselves.

It took emotionally painful years, but writing helped me figure out what I was really feeling deep down. It was anger, despair and, later on, shame. Telling myself to let go of those feelings didn't work and I wasted years dwelling on it and, worst of all, I was never compassionate with myself; I hated myself. I needed a creative outlet to let go of the traumatic experience and find my authentic self again.

Rain or shine, I walked over to the library basement and continued the process of writing, to the point that the bullies became nothing but a smoke cloud, disappearing into thin air. What I know for sure is that anyone who gets through bullying and abuse is a miracle, and to speed things along and stop wasting your own life because others made it miserable, find an outlet to let go. Your happiness lies within you and your actions. There are so many different characters in this life, and we can't get on with everyone, but we can make the decision to mind our own business and move on. It is pointless seeking revenge, but we can't help our emotions. We just have to control them, and not let them dictate our actions.

Writing is one of the best ways to speak through your work, stay rational, show initiative, grow your network and, at the same time, redirect the focus of the bad behaviour of bullies and abusers. As with anything in life, if you are not happy about something that has happened to you, or *is* happening, you need to make a decision about how you are going to change it. If you make the decision to write, especially about your painful experiences, it allows you to find networks, resources and ideas to change your entire life.

In creativity there is no room for revenge. The best strategy is to not show any sign of distress. Move yourself out of the situation and gain perspective elsewhere by building connections, and then showcase their bad behaviour through more professional communication.

I remember panic washing over me like a cold sea wave. I felt physically sick; every part of my body going cold and still. The bullies, who tormented me for all those years, were posting an anti-bullying campaign trying to progress their own agenda. The worst bullies, pretending to have any kind of compassion, and I was seeing right through them. My stomach shifting and cramping, my legs weak and shaky, I felt like life was methodically torturing me all over again. I told myself to look away and believe that somewhere out there was that protective charm against the stresses of victimhood.

Instead of crawling back to my bed and underneath the covers, feeling the world's darkness all around, I decided to pick up my pen and write. I reminded myself to: shift the focus from others onto myself, not allow them to have tremendous power over my wellbeing, make a decision to focus on better things and take responsibility for my feelings. I was the one holding resentment, feeling angry and allowing them to make me feel bad years later. I was never going to inspire and empower people around me feeling like that, and that was the moment I made the decision to move on. If the same bullies were going to haunt me in the future, I would sigh and look away, for good.

Don't underestimate how much you know. Your gift can be your story and the wisdom you hold in your heart. We have to bring ourselves to the table if we want to win and realise that trapped feelings can rule our emotional states, even without us being aware of them. Writing can bring that awareness and let the emotion express itself, so you can let it go. You may also doubt the importance of your written work, and the impact it may have on the world, but art and expression matter and our world would not be the same without them.

Find your champions

We are all given a little bit of creative madness, and if we end up using it, it might bring us unexpected joy. I see this in my daughter, and I tell her to use her creativity as much as she feels like.

From early on in our lives, we are told to shut our feelings down; "Don't cry," we tell little children. Suffocating our feelings just because they are dark and sad causes us more long-term negativity. We need to go into the darkness and feel it. We need to understand and recognise our pain.

I took tablets to combat the feelings of pain from being bullied. Lodging emotional pain deeper in my body created a negative thinking process that rushed to the surface after I stopped taking the medication. My own thoughts started to create more and more suffering. If I had dealt with my feelings of being bullied and learned to become more assertive, my thought process would never have got so negative and left me with the stuck thoughts.

The internal investigation I should have done was pushed aside by the tablets that made me feel nothing. To be conscious is to be sad; the pain is necessary for the creative process. I look up to Frida Kahlo. She felt enormous physical and mental pain, yet she decided to establish herself as self-sufficient.

I stopped the tablets, slowly feeling like myself again; even with the pain and negative thinking that now rushed to the surface. I started to write, every day. I fell in love with the process of writing, and this is when I started to see real results. The writing process not only gives clarity, but also takes away the anger.

We often start by seeing everything in a twisted way when we have been hurt, and through my own writing, I recognised how I placed the characters and scenes. It's not controversial to say that you can always kill your enemies off in your novels. It's a much better solution than hurting yourself. My dream is to find champions; those people with strong, loyal values who are there for the bullied, who step up, defend and support when people need it most. These champions could save lives. They could change your outlook and make you realise that you haven't been programmed for a negative, downward spiral for life just because someone bullied you. We tend to be intensively practical and analyse everything, forgetting the unexpected. It's impossible for the bullies to control everything; especially a changed you.

Another problem when we are in a negative state is that we tend to attract the wrong types of people, work and lifestyle. The champion people by your side will encourage you to walk away from these things.

During the time I was knocked down, I accepted the wrong type of work, or no work at all, and clung onto friends despite the way they behaved, until I had my own awakening and realised I'm too old to be talking to someone, knowing it's leading nowhere. It's best to have people around you who encourage dedication and focus back on your life. Think of an actor who does his own stunts. This actor needs dedication and focus to fully immerse into the role, instead of using a body double. Chances are, whilst doing his stunts he is having the time of his life.

Champions can be the reason someone feels seen, heard and supported, whilst bullies are the reason someone feels insecure, negative and sad. Champions can also empower the victim; make you accountable and help you focus on the things you can control.

Successful champions have one thing in common: they all embrace failure and believe there are many opportunities in this world; enough for everyone. Therapeutic writing can be soothing for your painful emotions, and for me, it was an eye-opening experience. Every day in that library basement, I took myself on a journey of enlightenment, and with this book, I want to get my message out: it's ok to get angry, but it's not ok to be cruel. We can't expect everyone to like us and often it's the bullies' own insecurities and history that stop them seeing the best in you and make them turn cruel. Even after being severely bullied, when you accept yourself again and find your creative power, you are invincible. The pain gives you understanding and when we own our story, we also own the ending. This is the power of creative therapeutic writing. The perfect balance for me came from writing the emotions down, but not worrying about perfection. It's about gaining control of your emotions, rather than perfection in writing. If you make the effort to do your best, that's already success.

Creating your own deadlines, motivation and productivity is also success. Sometimes the driving force to write happened when I felt intensive emotional pain in my chest. I needed to get it out. If I wanted to write but was struggling with productivity, I used to work 25 minutes, have a five minute break and repeat.

Unless we get the emotions out somehow, when our emotional balance is off, it can end up destroying us. No one dies from a snake bite alone. It is the venom that continues to pour through your system after the bite that ends up destroying you. This is bullying and abuse; it is not the attack, it's the aftermath in your head. If we get the emotions out and have supporting champions around us, they can prevent the poison from destroying us.

Journaling ideas

When my surgeon asked me to write a 'pain diary,' I wasn't sure how to start. Doctors should be relying on the idea that science is the most powerful form of evidence; blood tests and scans, not me badly describing my dying bones and chronic pain, with English as a second language and no knowledge of the medical terms.

Then it occurred to me that when we have suffered trauma, any kind of writing will help us get to the source and see the damage caused by long-term exposure to negativity. The same applied to my physical pain; the pain diary provided clarity of the situation to all involved. Your writing doesn't need to be complex. Simple journaling of our thoughts allows us to be more successful, as we allow inspiration to flow again, bringing back hope and motivation. Writing, whether a journal, novel or just a list, gives us a way to let go of all the trapped emotions and overthinking; the wisdom in us will start to shine.

One of the greatest ways to reconnect with yourself in a simple way is through journaling. I think of it as interviewing myself and ask a range of questions regarding my intentions and actions, from "What is my vision?" and "How do I attract this to my life?" to "What is my next step in turning this vision into reality?"

Writing things down clears our minds, and also gives us an idea of what to let go. If it doesn't appear in your writing, is it even part of your life? The key is to trust your inner voice and your awareness.

It took me a while to find that courage again, from deep inside my soul, to start living on my own terms. I never wanted to settle for an easy existence, for a life that blends into one big blur, leaving no legacy behind. I looked back on all my yesterdays, all my achievements, all those things I found meaning in, and I knew none of it was for nothing. I wasn't going to let bullies and abusers trap me into a meaningless life. I had university degrees, corporate careers and countless travels behind me. I had been mentoring work colleagues and friends and I was proud of how I made people feel, and what I could still put out into the world. It wasn't over.

I started to write a journal titled 'Self-Rescue for Beginners.' It was only for my benefit, and I addressed how to recover from some of the devastating experiences of life.

Journaling is surprisingly revealing as a form of writing therapy, because journals are not to be read by anyone else. We can freely write about the pain and depth of loneliness whilst staring into the abyss of "Who am I?" without the fear of making uncomfortable reading.

Have you ever frozen in terror as you walked out of a shop and set the alarms off on the way? The security guards running towards you, hunting through your every pocket and bag whilst people stare and judge you like you are the thief of the century, when you were looking for something you couldn't even find, didn't touch anything and certainly didn't steal anything. Yet here you are, all of a sudden, being treated like a criminal. This is life; we can be lugging something around that sets alarms off without even realising it.

Dealing with trauma is never easy or pleasant, but it needs to be done. Through my journal, I was reflecting on my painful journey and realised that I was simply preparing myself for something even worse. Life, for me, wasn't 'living in the present moment.' It was like being too scared to enter a shop because I knew I would set the alarms off, even without touching anything.

Physical pain knocks you down without your consent. Mental pain lingers in multiple layers, for as long as you let it. I had already experienced moving to a different country, starting over, abuse and bullying, loss of income and disability. I was waiting for the other shoe to drop. I was certain that these times would define who I was by how I responded, and I wanted to be ready. I was always certain that something bad was coming to cancel out the good. Victimhood had taken over me and I was struggling with the idea that, actually, you can be happy all the time and you deserve to be. You can experience abundance and love and the best is yet to come.

Looking back on all my writing for 'Self-Rescue for Beginners,' I realised that I was only human. I had been too occupied with the 'danger just around the corner' concept, too scared to log on to social media in case the abusive words were there, multiplying like a noxious weed, too scared to have my photo taken by anyone in case it was posted online and gave proof of my existence.

After my turning point, I realised that I had evolved from a time when I did have to pay attention to danger around the corner. By writing 'Self-Rescue for Beginners,' I was really preparing myself to evolve out of that victim mentality, and when I finally did, it was proof that we can prepare ourselves to recover from anything we choose, by writing about it. Now when I find myself thinking that the other shoe is about to drop, I change my mindset by reminding myself that I have already evolved from living in fear. I have also evolved with my journaling; from self-rescue themes I have moved on to finding ways to reconnect with myself, manifest good things into my life and think about the outcomes of my ability to deal with problems. If you have been journaling for a while, your past journals will help you to deal with any future issues. You know you can grab the pain and suffering from those pages and turn it into useful wisdom.

Journaling connects you with yourself, reminds you who you are, and is a perfect opportunity to make yourself a priority. Write about yourself and your life. It's not selfish. It's necessary. Journaling helps you to stay in your own lane. You can use simple writing prompts such as: "I remember when," "My happiest memory" or "Today my pain feels like" to get you started.

We grow by being vulnerable. Bullying made me protect myself and my image too much, but it was the initial journaling that made me step up. As a practice, you can try writing a journal called 'Flow some.' Describe yourself as an individual who embraces their flaws and knows they are awesome regardless. By pulling all your energy and focus back towards yourself will help you towards authentic and happy life. If you are fighting with anxiety, look at the bright side of your pain; shift the focus to realise that we all have stories to tell. I used journaling to deal with bullying through strategic planning as well. Through this journal I set specific goals and objectives. It also helped me to get ready for changes in response to the shifting dynamics that happen in life.

In regards to cyber bullying, my strategy journal looked like this:

1) Screenshot and save everything

2) Communicate to trusted people what is happening. Do not keep this to yourself

3) Do not retaliate. It is what they want

4) Block

5) Check security settings

6) Repeat (as I am prepared for new accounts appearing with the same tactics)

Specific Goals:

Concentrate on other matters and surround yourself with positive and happy people

No matter what, do not let them get to you

Objectives:

Start loving what you do

And then, I decided to change my strategy! Why go with the safe option? Is that going to help me? Is it going to help me get over the pain and hurt, or grow as a person? My answer was no, and I decided to write down (remember, write everything down as it gives you clarity) my other choice. This was the one that was scaring me the most, but I knew it would help me in many ways. This strategy was about speaking up. Speak the truth with kindness, and let it flow. As in my case, if someone is constantly aggressive and rude and makes you feel small, it's time to speak up. I hate confrontation, but now I know that there is something I hate even more, and that is feeling constantly sad and letting bullies win. I also needed something other than strategic planning, because living life like a business plan is draining. Living life in a flow is the opposite; you can relax into it and live in the now.

Journaling can help you to live in the moment by trusting your inner guidance system. Most of my stress and anxiety came from the way I was responding and what I was focusing on, not life itself. By communicating your truth into existence with the flow, no matter how painful, you are not only transferring it, you are thinking it through, processing and preparing not to let emotional abuse slowly chip away at you. Negative self-perception will disappear and self-esteem will come back when you simply feel capable of communicating.

Writing things down in the journal gave me clarity and after I stopped worrying about the strategies and went with the flow, I realised that the struggle had been with my creative mind. No matter how hard we try, some of us can't think in a linear way.

Ideas for writing and where to get them

Negativity is a killer for the creative mind. Becoming aware and switching your thoughts from negative to positive is the first step for great ideas to start flowing. Even the most successful writers feel doubt and uncertainty when starting a project. It's only natural to feel this way, but what successful writers have is perspective.

As a trauma sufferer, you have already overcome the odds; you already have perspective without even knowing it. Stepping into the writing greatness and discovering the creative world of ideas and inspiration allows you to overcome all the negative internal self-talk by being aware of your thoughts and finding your perspective again.

Sometimes writers focus on literacy but forget about the emotional value readers get from stories. Trauma sufferers who have come out of the grips of their pain forget that they left so many things untouched whilst struggling to survive. Having been disabled in spirit, it's not a bad idea to have an uneventful period for purpose of reflecting. It's also fine to try and find the reason why bad things happen to us, but as a writer, don't get obsessed with this one idea for too long. Get it out and move on.

Ideas can come from nature all around us; from flora and fauna, landscapes, urban architecture and the countryside, inland and out from the sea.

Your thoughts inspire action, and that's the compass that matters when brainstorming. Your thoughts need to be clear. You can't bury unexpressed emotions beneath new ideas. They will always come forth somehow and the solution is to heal by expressing. I took thoughtful action in the direction that mattered to me. Meanwhile, the cyber bullies did what they always do. They were updating statuses and ranting online, appeasing their egos. They are still the same. I changed. The old me disappeared as my journey shifted and I began to transform and leave behind my old mindset. It can happen quickly and clearly like a shooting star, but for me it took the length of the first writing process.

Ideas come when you are flexible and journey-minded. Find the strength and courage to share your ideas. I believe we can all be naturally gifted storytellers if we only try and enjoy it. Ideas and brainstorming will come easily if we drop the passive-participant act and realise that, to overcome unexpressed emotions, we need to forge ahead. Sometimes you need to drop negative people and start following those who are several steps ahead of you. They might have gone through trauma similar to yours. Pick up their way of thinking and watch what they do.

You were put on this earth to do astonishing things. And, to do so, you need to shift the focus to have ideas and brainstorm, but it is hard to motivate the brain and eliminate negative energy blocks when you are feeling depressed, traumatised and sad.

I tried a range of different writing styles. Then, I improved and expanded my daily routine with consistency. If you want to progress, consistency is the key. Once you are in the flow of writing, keep on going. Writing is an isolating activity in itself, but it also helped me disrupt the patterns that sapped my energy and isolated me. How? I felt the need to get out there to brainstorm and look for ideas for my writing.

We all begin our creative journey from an ambiguous place and we can all harvest ideas from life around us, no matter who or where we are. Try not to focus all your writing on the pain you have been through or turning points in life.

I also thought about what I truly loved about life and what inspired me. I had always been drawn to travel, fashion and style. It felt easy to write about these things because I didn't have to put in as much of my emotions.

I was writing travel articles and realised I was taking too long with one piece. It wasn't due to lack of motivation, as travel writing is one of my favourites, it was because I was aiming for it to be perfect and kept editing to the point where I was rewriting everything. I decided to set myself a goal; to finish a written piece by the end of the week.

To hold myself more accountable for my travel writing, I used a metaphor. Your metaphor can be anything that relates to your writing. A metaphor, like a powerful affirmation, can increase the power of the subconscious mind to kick start the writing process. I used 'ETA' for travel articles. Planes are expected to land at their 'estimated time of arrival.' Sometimes they fly off course due to unexpected circumstances, off the specific flight plan, and explanation is needed. It also made me think of my writing as a flight plan. We often encounter writer's blocks and come off course. Thinking about the metaphors, even subconsciously, directed me back to writing; back to the 'flight plan.' By way of comparison, like the pilot of the plane, I was held accountable for achieving my destination, despite coming off course.

As well as metaphors and comparisons are helping you to get your writing done, visualising the day when the writing is finished helps you stay on course. Visualise to feel good and create a strong momentum. There is also always an opportunity to see how successful people do things, but better than that is to read stories about failure. These are rare, as everyone loves to talk and write about their success (although success is a very relative concept) but if you are lucky enough to find a good story about failure, don't let it go; learn from it. Failure is a great teacher and spawns creativity. Writing about failure is emotional and might not come easily to everyone, but it instils courage and builds character more than any other type of writing. For me, it never came easily, but after each emotional story was finished, I felt relief. I went outside and noticed the small things. The green grass. Nature. I started to source other ideas from the simple life around me. I realised that to get to this stage, I needed to write the painful emotions away, and by doing this, I trained my mind to be stronger than my emotions. I was not going to lose myself ever again. I was now able to harness ideas from life around me and my thinking became specific, intentional and particular. I started to think more optimistic thoughts and my battles slowly turned into blessings as I discovered the true gift of writing.

If you start to feel passionate about writing and it naturally evolves, you may want to take it to the next level. At this level, you can consider hiring a reliable editor who is consistent with your original intent and helps you with continuity.

Writing helps you to define your unique value. Writing with consistency, reinforcement and repetition or a common theme across your writing will help you shape your own author brand. Author brand is about building a relationship with your readers and your future growth as a writer. You can start creating your brand story by writing down what motivates you to write, your strengths as a writer, what types of reader will find value and emotional connection in your writing and what steps you will take to build meaningful relationships with your readers.

II

PRACTICAL SAMPLES FOR INSPIRATION

Point of view – who is telling your story?

When you start writing, the first thing to consider is the point of view of your story. There are several to select from, but the most commonly used are first person subject narration and third person limited, or subjective. In the first person, 'I' tells the story. You can see this type of narration in most of my writing examples, but I have added a third person sample, below. If you are writing about traumatic experience, the third person perspective can be used to escape personal feelings. Write as if you are narrating the life of a stranger.

There are advantages and disadvantages to both points of view. As a writer, you can play around with both before finding the right one for you. Below is a sample of my writing, in third person. If you would like to practice point of view writing, rewrite the short story below in first person.

Writing in third person sample

'Night at New Cross'

The rain had been pouring all afternoon and the sky had darkened to the same boring grey as the wet slate rooftops. Harriet made her way out of the top deck of the bus, pushing and shoving, as if trying to get out of a sardine can. Standing on the side of the road, she almost fell backwards on the uneven pavement.

"Oi, watch it!" yelled a young man from the rain-streaked bus window as it splattered her with brown water from the gutters.

Harriet started slowly walking, her head down, darkness falling over the grey pavement, making everything appear black.

Suddenly someone shoved her from behind and was pulling her arm.

"Give me your bag!" a man with a black hoodie demanded.

"Just take it, here!" Harriet threw the bag on the wet ground and started backing off. The shiny silver end of a sharp blade was circling left, right, left, right, in front of her shocked eyes. One single rain drop landed on the blade, mesmerising Harriet. Completely frozen, she stood still as the man ran away.

People getting off at the bus stop hurried past. No one said a word.

After a while, Harriet stared at the empty street, her coat drenched. Lights came on in the nearby buildings. Her hands were shaking and she was shivering. A tear rolled down her cheek. She looked up at the tall buildings flicking their lights back on, wiped salty tears from her cheeks and started walking. She felt angry, insulted and enraged.

"Rise above it... rise above it..." She bit her lip and walked faster.

She kept telling herself it was only a handbag. "What was in that bag, anyway?" She started smiling. "Bag of pine nuts that had been there a week, a leaking pen that was taken from the hotel conference room, a bus pass that's not valid, a rusty key that doesn't work unless you yank it, a flavoured water bottle mixed with laxatives, a five-page dossier from the boss regarding the reasons why there is no money left for the Christmas party this year..."

The further Harriet walked, the more the robbery became a laughable and ridiculous memory.

Travel writing

We have all stumbled upon a great adventure at some point in our lives and I'm not necessarily talking about exotic holidays. This could be a misadventure in your own neighbourhood. Don't write to impress if you are writing for an audience; all you have to do is engage the reader with your own unique voice, with a quest in mind.

Below you can find two short travel stories where I used simple memories and feelings as narrative building blocks.

'Travelling Game'

As the sun is slowly spreading its gleaming tendrils into every corner of the train carriage, making it cosy and warm, I feel the kick of the train moving along. I feel warm inside, and safe. "God, I love trains," I whisper. I see another train moving along outside the window with a sign that catches my eye; *Destination: Paris.* I haven't been to Paris since *that* trip.

Paris is always going to bring me contradictory feelings; recollections of my stupidity and fear, but also the admirable struggle to preserve personal integrity and a lesson learned.

Most people say that Paris should not be described, it should be felt. I still feel the panic of being chased through the slippery cobblestone streets under a thin drizzle, discomfort in my chest, my voice echoing as I call through the iron bars.

As the memories come flooding in, I realise there is no point dwelling on why things went badly. We didn't seek to flirt with danger and it wasn't Paris that was meant to hurt us consciously, it was simply a bad person.

I met Helen at a party. She was tanned and slender, with red wavy hair and strikingly pale blue eyes. A sense of curiosity fell upon the room as she entered; all voices hushed and movement paused at the poker table. Her presence was startling and when she floated in to the kitchen to get more drinks, I followed her.

We stood in front of each other, eyes searching with excitement, faces bright with anticipation as to who would speak the first word. She offered me M&Ms and told me in a gentle voice that her mother died recently and that she didn't really like sharing her M&Ms with anyone but her mother. I could be an exception. She used to go and sprinkle them at her grave, leaving her a few.

I told her about my parents, who had gone trekking in the mountains, and that's when she brought up her desire to travel. Just like me, she felt a calling; a deep anticipation in her bones to set off without delay, a plan or map.

Deep in conversation together, we were imagining the alluring departure boards, stunning views from the windows and the rhythmic swaying of trains. We started obsessing about trains and how we could cross countries with the opportunity to stop whenever we wanted, stay over for a night or two, or sleep on the night trains.

Reminiscing, I am surprised by how strongly I still feel it all. Starting from the miraculous feeling of sucking in the life around us like sponges, enjoying every second. I can almost feel Helen's soft, humid breath, the air quietly rising from her nostrils as the metal train wheels turned on the train track, the loud flange squeal hurting my ears. I close my eyes as I summon my memories and drift back to that dusky night in July, 1992:

Helen starts coughing in her sleep. I rub my watery eyes, feeling light-headed.

Helen wakes up, her tired gaze lingering on our large backpacks. Disorientated, we step out onto the platform.

After all the spontaneous fun in Amsterdam, we haven't even planned the next stop; no place to stay, no maps. Being spontaneous is part of the fun on our European tour and every second of this trip I've had the blissful feeling of not letting life escape us, but sucking it in with passion.

Stepping outside the train station, I blink in disbelief. It's dark and raining and we are exhausted. "Don't you think we should turn around?" I whisper to Helen, motioning back to the safety of the seventeenth century station.

"And what? Sleep on the platform?" she snuffles, looking ahead.

I reflect on the good times we had in Amsterdam, the random hotel we found and all the new friends we made.

"Chicken!" she mocks.

We walk along the cobbled streets with our heavy backpacks. An older man sets his eyes on us from the shadows of a late-night Paris café. He stares, his thick black eyebrows rising, and I become aware that you can tell by our unkempt appearance that we have been backpacking for a while.

The man starts talking in French, fast, his arms swinging, trying to seem welcoming. I already regret making eye contact with him, but we recognise the word 'hotel' as he makes gestures of sleeping.

I follow Helen's gaze to the man and understand that she wants to go to the hotel. Something feels off, but he chats on, oblivious to the time. Our eyes flicker involuntarily; we are struggling to concentrate.

He starts leading us through the narrow yellow cobblestone streets, the night getting darker and the rain heavier. Wrapped around a cobbled courtyard we see a row of seventeenth century buildings, one with a flashing 'Hotel' sign. His laugh, throaty and loud, echoes in the air.

We follow him inside and the wind slams the door shut. It's silent around the small reception desk, with an elderly man giving us a quick glance behind a newspaper. He talks slowly in French and hands over a key. To the man. He is swinging the key in the air like he has won the lottery and motions us to climb up five flights of dark, uncarpeted stairs with rooms deposited along the way. I stand in the doorway, indicating that I would rather check us in, pulling a small, colourful stack of bills out of my pocket. The man is already halfway up the bare staircase. Helen follows him without question and every single step up feels long and torturous. I stop to catch my breath, feeling annoyed.

He is yanking open the ancient door to the dark attic room. As it opens, we can see a dim street light beaming through the window that stretches to the roofline.

The man offers to help Helen take her backpack off as she steps into the room. I can tell that he is itching to touch Helen, to have his old hands on her. He lightly touches her back and I can see her body tighten, her face turning into a cringe. He signals for us to move further in, to explore the room, but I refuse, whilst holding onto the door frame.

My eyes sweep over the room and he gazes at me in surprise with his brown eyes, mostly hooded to hide his dark thoughts. He is guarding the door on the other side and when I ask him politely to pass me the key and wait outside, his nostrils flare and his hands close into fists. The next thing I know, he is holding me down, grasping my throat, tightening his grip to the point where I'm soon to cease all movement.

I see a glimpse of terror in Helen's tired eyes, realising she is trapped inside as the man slurs unintelligible words in French. He transfers his gaze calmly to Helen and loosens his grip.

And then, with all my weight, I lurch forward, hitting his head against the door, and yell at Helen to run.

He stumbles as he feels the blood draining from his face. He lurches towards us again and we push down the staircase with no hesitation. My feet slip and I almost tumble over.

We make it out to the middle of the cobblestone square with our chests heaving rapidly from the heavy panting. We punch away further into the darkness, the cobblestone street slippery underfoot.

With adrenaline pulsing, heaving lungs and palpitating hearts, we hide around the corner, finding refuge in the darkness.

Exhaustion dragging at our eyelids, we kneel down on the wet ground behind a Romanesque church. The cold air seizing our bodies, we breathe quietly, praying he is not lurking in the shadows.

I have no time to be angry at Helen for what might have cost me my life.

The rain settles into a light drizzle and suddenly we are facing the blue light from a police car swirling in the street.

We take a brave step forward, back to the square.

I wave my arms and the next minute we are talking too fast, in English, about the hotel and the man, the train station and Helen's backpack, which we left behind. I feel jittery, my eyes are wild and my pupils dilated. Heart racing, I reach for my backpack, but the police officer, with a strong jaw and brash eyes, grabs it. I have hidden my traveller's cheques and passport in a pouch under my clothes. Another officer taps me on the shoulder and motions for me to hand over my pouch. He calls to the officer with brash eyes and they pull our arms behind our backs into handcuffs. The cuffs are too tight, the chains too short. We stare at each other in disbelief.

We are shoved into the back of a police van. We sit there, catching our breath and listening. They are awfully quiet throughout the entire drive. My anxiety begins to ripen into bewilderment as our chained hands clatter against the side of the van.

We are dragged inside the tiny, cold police station and taken down the corridor to the holds that remind me of my grandmother's chicken cages in her basement. There are large holes in the beige concrete walls and we are soaked from the rain and shivering. They have taken our passports and my backpack and we are sure that Helen's backpack is still inside that spooky attic.

Hours pass. We watch random people come and go. Some look like they have been in the wars; holes in their jumpers, dirt on their faces and some with blood on their hands. "Murderers," I whisper to Helen.

I call through the bars, to anyone who will listen, "Anyone speak English? Can I use a phone? I need to make a phone call!"

I don't even know who I would call. Definitely not home.

A great, painful silence comes down and I step away from the bars. I desire fresh air.

A homeless Parisian tries to engage in conversation, half in French and half in English, and surprisingly the conversation is easy and relaxed, just like the person seems to be.

"Offal, offal, offal…" he repeats, shaking his head, not understanding why we are locked up. He is the total opposite of the man who took us to the hotel.

I stare at the homeless guy. So Parisian. So rustic and grotesque, but still chic.

I wonder if this absurd night in Paris has changed me.

I silently pray that the police don't write the bad guy off as just an obnoxious character. His intentions were not good and we can only hope he is not on the lookout for other unsuspecting, naïve travellers. I feel angry and betrayed at the outrageousness of it all, but we should have known better than to venture out into the dark Paris night, following a strange man. We had been warned repeatedly, but felt like we were living our dream; being spontaneous and invincible. Maybe we just experienced a city where the perceived decadence and sleaze fuels violence.

I keep biting my dry lips. A drop of water would be great. I bet the homeless guy's stomach is growling. I wonder when he last had a plate of food. A dam of frustration inside me bursts.

"Awful, awful, awful…" I say.

I decide to yell through the bars one last time. This time, I'm copying the homeless guy and his Parisian accent. "Offal!"

Homeless guy smirks, the corners of his eyes crinkling. I step closer to him. He has probably lived three days in one. We had one night of 'offal' and he has probably had a lifetime, or at least a very long time, judging by his unkempt appearance. And here I am judging him, just like the man judged us by trying to imprison us. Probably kill us, even.

As I approach the homeless guy again, he mumbles something in French and I imagine he is saying "Come sit with me, no agenda… just you and me talking about how strange the world is and what we are actually doing here…"

His voice is kind, and like two bilingual children code-mixing, we end up in conversation together, in French and English. I find out that he used to work as a builder and travelled the world. He comes from a big family. When discussing the topic of life and the future, his eyes light up with ambition and optimism. He dreams of a family of his own one day. He has been searching for work but ended up in the wrong crowd. Times have been tough lately.

He seems kind, gracious and endearing.

Looking about at the emptying cell, the beige walls look so dependable and neutral. I am suddenly overwhelmed by it all. Deep down, an acute awareness of our stupidity makes me want to scream.

Helen plays with her long, wavy hair. She is looking at the wall, as if staring off into oblivion.

For a while we sit in our customary silence and my mind is being captivated by the events of the night, repeating them over and over again.

At first I don't even register it, but then I overhear the police officer calling our names.

For the longest seconds of my life, we stand in front of the bars and, driven by hunger and thirst, we wave a quick goodbye to the homeless guy and the chicken cages with beige walls.

Sitting in the back of the police van again, not knowing where they are taking us, I have a hunch they are driving us towards a place where safety prevails; back to the Central Train Station.

When the van doors open and a beacon of light hits our tired eyes, I smile. My cheeks begin to blush and a strike of embarrassment rushes through me as the officer with brash eyes hands us our passports and points us towards a train.

The yellow sign in front of the large, white TGV Lyria is flashing with the word: *Zurich*. There are no curtains or sliding doors you can pull closed or locks to keep the bad characters of this world out. Still, stepping into this cosily small carriage makes me feel safe. Sitting here, reflecting, I feel like I have been granted extra dreamy, transformational time in this life. As the movement of the train brings a sense of sanctuary, I look behind me, one last time. I see the sun rising behind the elegant historic buildings. I let the soft amber glow of the sunrise pour through my fingers as I quietly wave goodbye to the city, blending in soft colours of yellow and sudden daubs of red and orange. Then, just like a baby being rocked in a bassinet, I close my eyes.

'The Golden Leaves of Corfu'

The cypress-studded hills fly by as I speed along the small, winding road, tiny rocks flying behind me. I leave behind villages and sandy coves lapped by cobalt-blue waters as I reach the mountain. A thin strip of brown dust alters the horizon. I blink and blink again.

My eyes wide in horror, I squeal loudly as the dust gives way; a huge truck is coming towards me, head-on.

I turn the scooter to the left and end up rolling down the hill. The sound of crunching metal and flying rocks surround me as I hang on to the scooter moving below me.

I land sideways on the uneven ground, the scooter beside me, my knee bleeding; the rocks underneath me hurting every inch of my body.

It's a warm, late September afternoon. The colour of the leaves making their home on the ground makes the entire hill appear golden.

I sweep the leaves with my hand as I attempt to get up. My hands are trembling as I try to pull the scooter up, but my painful knee stops me.

I'm kneeling on the hill, covered in dirt, bumps, cuts and crazes.

I take my time and slowly manage to get up the hill.

Exhausted, I push the scooter along on the side of the rocky road, realising I was in the wrong. I was travelling on the wrong side of the road!

It feels like hours getting back to the scooter shop, and I keep swearing at myself for being so careless and stupid.

The shop owner sees me from a distance and walks up to the gate. For a moment he looks at me in surprise, then lowers his gaze to the scooter.

A wave of embarrassment rushes through me as I start to explain about the accident, my voice shaking and eyes on his damaged scooter.

"It's minor anyway," he says with a sympathetic voice, and I see no signs of frustration in his eyes.

He tells me to sit on the white concrete veranda while he takes the rattling scooter in.

A breath of deep warm saffron lingers in the air as he walks towards the veranda with a tray of two steaming glasses of tea.

He sits beside me and offers me Sideritis; ancient Greek mountain tea, known for its anti-inflammatory benefits.

As the warm tea calms my trembling nerves, I realise how lucky I am. Nobody died; the golden leaves around me at the bottom of the hill were a sign that my future is only beginning.

I wipe the dry blood off my knee, take another sip of the enchanting tea and feel enormous gratitude.

Screenwriting

Writing a novel can be very different experience to writing a screenplay. I found that my writing process was more organised, structured and disciplined when I attempted my first screenplay. Screenplays need to work together with synopsis, character notes, outline and treatment (a summary of a script explaining the main plots, often written in present tense). When writing a novel, I was so obsessed with just writing, I ignored the structure of the story. The timeline needed editing, the characters had flaws and the story narrative didn't flow easily. I was jumping from time and place and the entire concept kept changing as I progressed. Not only did it become a nightmare to edit at a later stage, but I don't think anyone would have been able to enjoy reading it.

Learning screenwriting changed me as a writer. It made me think about the practical flow of the narrative and how to structure the manuscript from the beginning.

The length of a screenplay is shorter than a novel, which can act as a good 'work in progress' for a novel later on.

The example below shows the elements involved in writing a fictional screenplay.

Synopsis:

Case 131

"*Something happened in the past that should not have happened, and I resent that. If that hadn't happened, I would be at peace now.*" Harriet

"*She sleepwalked into the mountain stream of blood and sorrow.*" Johan

St Thomas' Hospital, London, January 2018. Harriet has been hospitalised for fainting and unexplained vision loss. The time in the hospital goes slowly, and at times when she feels clear-headed, she starts to write. The truth can get muddled up in her auras of eternal zigzags. She kept the painful secret for 30 years.

St Thomas' Hospital nurse, Gelda, checks on her patient. Gelda finds the notebook on the floor. Harriet asks her to read the first few pages out loud. She hesitates, but Harriet seems upset and in pain, so she opens the notebook. The title 'Case 131' sparks her curiosity and she starts reading. Harriet was just ten years old and travelling with her father, Johan, to Denmark, stopping over in Stockholm. She thought they were just going on holiday, but her father was transporting illegal firearms to be shipped to conflict zones.

Harriet used to regularly sleepwalk as a child and on the night of 28th February 1986, she sleepwalks again. She walks into a wooden box on the floor. She opens it up and it's full of guns. She picks a small black handgun and runs outside. It's quiet and no one is watching. She pulls the trigger and fires. Twice. The Prime Minister and his wife are walking towards the underground train station after spending the evening watching a play. The first bullet hits the Prime Minister, killing him. The second injures his wife.

The gun kicks back so hard that Harriet flies backwards. Johan hears shots being fired and hurries after Harriet. It's too late. He is limping due to a previous knee injury and can't get there fast enough. Harriet's ears are ringing and she runs towards the dark tunnel. Johan is holding her hand.

In the aftermath of the shooting, witnesses claim they saw a man limping near to the murder scene.

After her shift at the hospital, on the way home, Gelda passes by the City Library. She decides to put her doubts to rest and finds herself surrounded by history books. She discovers that the shooting Harriet wrote about is true;

in 1986, Prime Minister Olof Palme was shot one night on his way home. Despite his widow identifying a suspect and 130 people confessing to the murder, it is still one of the greatest unsolved mysteries.

Is Harriet just number 131, confessing to a murder that wasn't committed by her? No witnesses came forward seeing a child running around in a night gown.

The following night, Gelda returns for her shift, only to find out that Harriet has been put into a coma. *"Cerebral anerurysm"* she reads in Harriet's hospital files.

As she is going through the files she finds her next of kin. Harriet has left her father's number, and Gelda makes the call. No one picks up and she leaves a voicemail.

Days go by and Harriet remains in a coma. Gelda starts suspecting the murder story was just Harriet's imagination, after going through her medical history. Harriet has been medicated for delusions before and she stopped taking the medication two weeks ago.

Harriet's father, Johan, suddenly turns up. Gelda faces a dilemma; should she forget about it all or find out the truth from Johan?

One night she goes to check on Harriet and Johan is sitting by her hospital bed, quiet. He looks sad. Gelda hesitates, but he surprises her by asking her to join him in a prayer. Gelda agrees, and together they kneel next to her bed, quietly praying for her.

Gelda rearranges the bedside table and Harriet's notebook falls on the floor. Johan picks it up and flicks through it. He takes a step back and replaces the notebook. Gelda can't hide her feelings. Johan stares at her in the dimly-lit room. Gelda quietly asks Johan if everything in the book is true. Johan stays silent and walks away.

Character notes

Harriet, 41, has lived an uneventful, lonely life in the city of London. She has avoided making friends or having a family. She chose a lonesome career as a court room typist.

One day she faints in the court room after a decade of suffering from severe headaches and occasional vision loss. She is hospitalised, and in the hospital she writes her confession for one of the highest profile murders in the world; that of Swedish Prime Minister Olof Palme in 1986.

Gelda, 35, is a nurse working in St Thomas' Hospital. Gelda finds her notebook and starts reading it. She returns the notebook the following day but finds Harriet has been put into an induced coma, leaving Gelda with a moral dilemma.

Johan, 65, is the father of Harriet. He is a former arms dealer, now antique dealer. He has lived a tormented life. He was buying illegal firearms the night of the murder. He no longer walks with a limp.

Outline

In 'Case 131,' the audience is shown the tragedy that arises from failures laid bare by protagonist actions. Harriet has lived her life being invisible, because of the one incident she was almost unaware of, and her father is tormented; a bad man whose actions not only caused a death, but tore many lives apart and brought a nation down. The story will end with compassion, and the audience will feel relieved that the secret is still intact.

Sample – 'Case 131', Act One

ACT ONE

FADE IN

INT. ST THOMAS' HOSPITAL – EARLY MORNING

CLOSE ON a pair of white heels, walking fast through the hospital corridor. A woman opens the door to a room, heads inside.

INT. HARRIET'S HOSPITAL ROOM – DAY (D1)

GELDA

And how are we today?

HARRIET startles a bit, then turns to find NURSE GELDA approaching with a big smile. Harriet breathes, forcing a frown as bright sunlight shines through vertical blinds.

A long, quiet beat as Harriet takes in her bleak surroundings – two beds, separated by a curtain, a side table with a medicine tray. Gelda stares at her, analysing...

Harriet manages a whisper.

HARRIET

Hi. My head...

Gelda stands in front of Harriet's bed. Harriet's head is resting on the pillow. She is weak, in visible pain.

GELDA

Whatever you need, I'm here to help. OK?

Harriet nods. Gelda presses on her arm delicately and wraps a blood pressure pump around it.

Harriet doesn't move. Gelda pumps the pressure, then lets the air go down. She lifts her arm to take the wrap away. Her elbow hits the medicine tray on the side table. The tray falls on the floor.

GELDA

Oh, I'm so sorry. Let me clear that up.

Gelda kneels on the floor, picks up the tray. And then, her eyes fixate on the notebook, open on the floor. She picks it up.

GELDA

I think this is yours?

Harriet stares at Gelda, debating whether to tell her the truth.

HARRIET

It was me.

A long beat. Gelda looks at her, confused.

Harriet looks back at her, tears now welling in her eyes…

GELDA

I'm sorry. I shouldn't ask… I'll just leave it right here.

Gelda places the notebook on the side table. She looks at Harriet, who looks like she really wants to get something off her chest. Gelda glances at the notebook's title.

CLOSE ON notebook. 'Case 131.'

GELDA

Is it the pain? Here, your tablet.

Gelda reaches her arm out to offer the tablet. Harriet quickly swallows it down, but tears keep running down her cheeks.

HARRIET

Please read the notebook. It's important.

GELDA

The doctor on duty might want to see you. If he has time for this ward…
(then)
It says, 'Case 131'? Is that something that's upsetting you?

Gelda hands the notebook back. Beat. Harriet is quiet and broken.

HARRIET

Please read it out loud. The first page.

Gelda looks at her, turning a page. She starts reading out loud.

GELDA

Stockholm, just before midnight on 28 February 1986. The Prime Minister and his wife are walking towards the underground train station after spending the evening watching a play.
(then)
What is this about?

HARRIET

Please. Go on.

Gelda looks at Harriet. It seems like she really needs to hear Gelda read it, so Gelda looks down at the page and presses on delicately.

GELDA

The girl looks at the large wooden box. She opens it up. The box is full of guns. She picks up a small black handgun with her little hands. It feels heavy.

She wants to keep it, for a little while. She hides the gun in her red night gown and runs outside. She goes 'boom boom' and dances around with it on the street. No one can see her. She pulls the trigger back. The gun suddenly kicks back so hard that she flies backwards. Her back hurts. It's cold and she is shivering. Her ears are ringing.

Gelda pauses. She checks on Harriet. The medication seems to be working and her eyes are closing. She carries on reading in a soft, quiet tone.

GELDA

The first bullet hits the Prime Minister, killing him. The second injures his wife.

The girl holds her hands over her ears. The ringing doesn't stop. And then a man walks over to her. He is limping. He takes her hand and they run towards a dark tunnel as fast as they can. It starts snowing.

DR OLIVER (50s, head of the ward) steps in, closing the door behind him.

GELDA

Patient is Harriet Henriksson, 41. Recent fainting and vision loss. Headaches for a decade. We ran a CT scan and the results are in the file.

Dr Oliver is listening to his stethoscope –

DR OLIVER

Patient notes, please?

Gelda pushes the notebook to the side and hands the patient file over. Harriet has closed her eyes.

DR OLIVER

I'm needed in the trauma room. I will see her tomorrow morning. Could you shut those vertical blinds please? And make sure she doesn't stop taking her medication.

He hands the patient file back and is out of the door as quickly as he came in. Gelda moves closer to Harriet and gently touches her arm.

GELDA

Harriet? Harriet? Can you hear me?

Harriet mumbles quietly but her eyes remain closed. Gelda walks over to the window and shuts the blinds.

HARRIET

Please take the notebook. Read it. Let's talk in the morning. *Please.*

Gelda startles, then turns to Harriet. Her eyes are open. She is staring at her in the dark room.

GELDA

I can't. I'm sorry.

HARRIET

Please. The world needs to know the truth.

Short stories

Writing short stories is perfect training ground for developing new characters and playing around with complex or strange story ideas for full-length novels or screenplays. Writing brief pieces is an adventure where you can lean into your artistic intuition through focusing on the theme and imagery.

'The Hidden Heart'

"Today we have gathered here to say farewell to George, and commit him into the hands of God…"

The wind gently blows the narrow sunlit window shut as the grey clouds take over the sky outside. I feel the warmth of my black cashmere cardigan as the priest raises his voice.

A strike of tiredness rushes through me as I watch my boyfriend, Thomas, sink into the gloomy atmosphere. I am fatigued after the long drive and the tiresome boredom of the never-ending country lanes. The taste of last night's gin and tonics still touching my throat, I wish I was back in London, my face planted hard into the warm sheets.

I watch her take a seat in front of us as a dozen needles dance their way across my forehead.

She crosses one leg over the other, slowly, and taps the church pew in front of her with her shiny stiletto heels.

"Who wears shoes like that to the funeral?" I whisper to Thomas.

"Shhhh…" he lowers his dark eyebrows at me as the service moves from earth to heaven.

"Lord, our God, you are the source of life. In you we live and move and have our being, by your Grace, lead us to your Kingdom…" the words echo as the cold air blows coarsely through the archaic church hall.

Shivering, I pull the sleeves of my cardigan over my cold hands. My head feels heavier and slowly gravitates towards my shoulder. I want to remain motionless until the headache has eased, the tight band around my head no longer squeezing tighter and tighter around my temples. As my eyes flicker into darkness, the shadowy figure of a woman smiles as she takes the seat beside me and nudges me with a skinny arm. She looks at me with her striking black eyes and whispers with a gentle voice:

"This is one absurd time you're alive in, but when was anything innocent and ordinary? It never really was an ordinary life out here, you see, as I sat cross-legged on the floor and begged a vicious ending for them. The room had no light, but I saw them fondling, kissing each other, mouth on mouth. He enjoyed the feeling of an eager mouth, the touch of a new girl. Impatient man. Her hair inches away from his nose, he rolled his eyes and nuzzled into her shoulder. I felt no fury or jealousy. I was gentle to my precious little soul, and silently drawn to the new calling that excited my spirit more than the man I learned to despise. These words, cursing, came out like a spitfire from my anguished and tormented soul, as my bones ached on the floor; "When lightning strikes, come all you demons, hear my call." They thought I was full of life and ideas, when death was apparent, and the ideas were all profanity. The carousel of thoughts, the precursor of obscenity, the blackness all over me. The carousel would never come to a stop, as they were endlessly cavorting.

I held the silver tea strainer behind my aching bones as he drank the liquid amber within the ivory bone china. I watched him go limp, and cradled him to my chest. I whispered in his ear: "I never thought you would be so pig-headed, Henry."

I cradled him harder and felt a fleeting moment of pleasure. He was like a cute animal, and I wanted to squeeze his little brains out. My emotions increased in complexity. My hands trembled with excitement and confusion, but I let go, on that decisive moment, and that was the death of me.

It's true I gave the tyrant strife, but in the end the life was his educator, as it was mine, and after agonising minutes, my consciousness ebbed, the carousel finally came to a stop. I became even more interesting for it, divisive even. To be beheaded, there's some pleasure in it. Your brain stays active, and that's when my soul stayed on the ground, forever. Why I sat beside you, you wonder. I lead you to the perception of more cues; men's carnal desires."

I wrench myself awake, slowly opening my eyes. The lady beside me gone, her long oval face and rather long nose disappeared. Whoever she was, she evoked something hidden and strange. "I must be dreaming," I say, holding a hand to my forehead and slowly lifting my head up. Thomas is not listening. He has his eyes captured on her slender, perfectly toned legs, her shiny black stockings contributing to their magnetic appeal. Her legs pleasing and teasing him from a distance. She knows what she is doing.

As the priest stops talking, Thomas suddenly turns his face to me, his dark chocolate eyes meeting mine, then facing forward again. My mind drifting, we all stand up and mutter our prayers.

It had been love at first sight, the day I met Thomas. The second I'd seen him our eyes had locked. Or so I thought. If I hadn't been so blind in the pink clouds of love, I would have stomped away in disgust as his gaze went from one to the other. He was barely aware of me, but I could have watched his charming ways forever.

As we move outside and stand watching George's casket being lowered into the ground, there isn't one inch of her body that doesn't intrigue him.

George laid to rest, I excuse myself and rush to get the bitter taste of gin and tonic out.

I leave the bathroom and stroll around the back garden of the church, looking for Thomas. I can almost hear the whispers, *"Time she came to her senses, he has been cavorting and wandering, poor girl hasn't had enough happiness."*

I glance over and see her spin around. She looks doubtful, for only a moment. He lays an arm across her shoulders, and briefly hugs her before kissing her flawless cheek. I back away, nothing about this making sense, my eyes flashing with indignation and anger, people staring. There are always witnesses to my misery.

The priest stops me. "You can go as far as you like, but a broken heart travels with you."

"I'm not going to fly off the rails. I'm astounded by his stupidity…" I motion towards the garden.

"I could weep and scream, and think of all the appropriate words of loss and hate, but is anything innocent and ordinary?" I put a fist in front of my mouth so that he can't smell the gin on my breath.

The priest looks at me, worried.

"I am not sorry for myself, just for what he'll do to her…" I say, agonising and wishing it was still last night. I had been sucking the lemon from my gin glass, Thomas beside me, thawing my anger and returning that innocent loving spark. Come to think of it, though, he felt so far away, lying by my side. Part of me wishes I'd never met him, and part of me wishes he was still by my side, kissing my lips, silencing all my questions.

"It is a vicious circle. Forgive them and forgive yourself." The priest intrudes on my contemplation with a soothing voice.

I tilt my head as if trying to predict what he will say next. "Typical priest… humble and respectful, devoted to his faith" I think to myself and refrain from rolling my eyes at him.

"Priests… giving guidance both on morals and in the means of persevering in the devout life, but could you pick the liars and players like Thomas out there?" I lash out with my lethal stare, painful and piercing. "I don't mean to be rude, but it's the half-truths which preceded it all. It's not the incidents like this, it's the lies," I add, lowering my gaze, scratching my sore head.

As the priest takes my hand, from the dark and ashen wall, a gloomy portrait of a drawn and pale face stares at me. I let go of his hand and take a step closer to the wall. "It's her!" My eyes are captured by her portrait. I stand there for a long, frozen moment. "Her name is Anne Boleyn. Wow." I look up at the memorial again with widened eyes, and quietly summarise the controversial story;

"She was crowned Queen but her time at the top was short-lived; her rise was as impressive as her fall sordid. She was executed, beheaded, with a sword. It all remains a mystery… was she a victim of a dreadful miscarriage of justice, beheaded

to make room for the new mistress, victim of an impatient man, or in fact, guilty as charged? Maybe behind closed doors she dabbled in sorcery and alchemy?"

I feel her in these walls. Her shapely eyebrows lead me to imagine her face slowly aging, her striking black eyes looking up with a friendly smile. "Did she admit secretly resorting to sorcery? What did she say again? Oh God, why am I so hungover!" I bite my lip in frustration. I remember her gaze, both amused and provocative, her great confidence and clarity of thought.

"You are not the only one to claim you've had an exchange with her discarnate soul." The priest stands behind me, his lips curled upwards. "Her heart is said to be buried in the crypt here."

"Do you believe her heart is really here?" I ask him in a husky voice as I study the portrait of Anne, her blank face, no fear in her eyes.

"Is her heart *really* buried in the crypt?" I repeat in admiration and amazement.

"Perhaps we will never really know, but I would like to believe her heart is here. It is a lovely thing for the parish. It encourages people to come to church," he says.

I settle back to look at the memorial again, and it now occurs to me that there was nothing between me and Thomas. We were poles apart, with nothing in common. He wasn't even a good listener.

"Thank you for talking to me, and listening…" I tell the priest and hover towards the red rug covering the entrance.

"I would like to pray for you," he says politely.

"There's no need to pray for me. Pray for them," I motion towards the church garden.

"Please tell Thomas, and that Jane Seymour over there, that I've gone," I say and spin around on the red rug, and for a moment I expect Anne to appear at the door to say goodbye and offer a few words of spiritual consolation.

As I swing the large door open, my breathing turns into white puffs in the crisp air of early spring. No wonder this place provided Anne with some of the happier times of her life; the life starting to blossom through the yellow daffodils as I keep on walking, and the birds chirp away as if to cheer me on. I allow the gentle breeze to brush my long locks across my face as I relish this ordinary moment, realising that the gifts of life, small to begin with, are stepping stones to greater.

I forgive his devious ways and leave him behind the stained-glass rose windows. Her presence and charm still inside, with that hidden heart, appearing for sad souls like me.

As I stop, one last time, to look over the terracotta roof tiles of the church, I whisper with the blowing wind: "Anne, times may always be crazy, but you can make them ordinary. Thank you, for opening my eyes to weed out the wrong one, the tainted soul. In my vulnerability, I found the sacred, hidden heart. I plan to finally plant my face into those warm sheets, and rest in peace. Hopefully you can, too".

'Island of Certainty'

Waiting in the hospital cancer ward, I've been scribbling on my notebook about eternal life. The strike of tiredness rushes through me as I watch my father sink into the gloomy hospital atmosphere. There is no healing, damage has been done, my father being pushed around between radiotherapy, fluoroscopy and various departments offering no way out. The pages of my red notebook start to live a story of transformation, offering a feeling of certainty where none exists;

Kneeling before the overwhelming dark sea, waves splashing, my ribs heave up. Both hands tightly holding the railing, I gasp for the salty air. With every wave I wheeze, like air escaping from a deflating balloon.

Suddenly, a gentle tap on my shoulder makes my spine shiver. An elderly man wearing a crisp, white, long agbada, a traditional long robe, motions towards the back of the vessel. I try to speak, but my stomach contracts violently. I purge colourful lava all over my shoes. I wipe at my mouth, acidic residue forming a shiny patch on my shivering arm. The hairs on my arm standing up. I'm about to sink to my knees.

Tears overwhelm my eyes, my head spinning. I lean over the edge, clenching my teeth tightly together. Strong waves throw bursts of cold murky water on my numb face. I sink behind the railing, only to catch the second spray of sea foam, salty water reaching the back of my tongue. I rub my watery eyes, squint and look around again. "Where is everyone?"

Rough waves slam over me without mercy. I stare at my shoes. The colourful lava disappears somewhere among the white sea-foam. I'm holding on to the railings for my life, whilst taking baby steps towards the back of the boat, trying not to fall on the slippery deck in the semi-darkness. "Where did the man go?"

The endless grey ocean around me, the soul of all colour, uniting with the grey clouds, looking darker by the minute. An icy cold raindrop lands on my shoulder as I pull myself off the deck, and with one forceful kick, the creaky back door opens.

The dark staircase groans as I go down, cobwebs entangled on the railing.

I enter a dimly-lit seating area, fear crossing my mind. This is no ordinary private boat or merchant vessel.

"Going to Carmine Island too?" a lady with a husky voice whispers, looking at me with her narrow, beaming red eyes. She is adjusting a dark purple silk scarf around her neck, covering red marks.

"Did you see a man with a white robe coming back from the top deck just now?" I ask, scanning the surroundings.

"Over there," her croaky voice escapes her lips. I see her shifting nervously in her seat.

I take a step further, trying to stay in line with the oncoming waves, an unsettling feeling welling inside me. "Where is this man? Disappeared like our memories?" My head tensing left and right, I scan the cabins until I see a dark shadow at the bridge, leaning over the helm.

"Hello, excuse me," I whisper.

He is hunching his back as I walk closer. I recognise him. "Hello, you saw me on the deck," I say a little louder.

He turns slowly, glancing me up and down.

"You don't remember?"

He shakes his head.

"It was only a short while ago. I was feeling sick. All those enormous waves hitting this vessel so hard."

"Well, I'm sorry." He sounds as apologetic as he does puzzled, avoiding eye contact. The ever-growing waves splash on the window. The boat is fast approaching large rocks. "Quick, take the helm!" I yell at him.

His vacant half-smile twisting his face, he freezes. I quickly grab the helm and steer away from the rocks. I elbow him and raise my voice.

"Hey wake up! I need you to direct this thing!" I elbow him harder. His dark skin is slowly turning pale and transparent, showcasing electric blue veins against his white robe.

Grabbing the helm, he slowly turns. He looks at me, bewildered, his face twisting into a scowl. He looks to be on the edge of his sanity as he moves his now chalky body closer and sinks his sharp teeth into my neck.

I take a deep breath and put my hands over my head, twitching my bloody, wet locks as my legs give way.

His shadow over my unconscious body, he quietly whispers my name, words falling endlessly into the ocean around us, mapping the secrets.

I can almost feel the crisp air battering my eyeballs as I open my eyes wide. I kneel to look through the narrow staircase going down.

"Where are we going?' I question him, as my human eyes are yet to see that I am actually wiping drops of blood off my neck without registering. Cold, crispy air between us, his skin no longer looks transparent. I can't see his electric blue veins. His vacant smile slowly returns, and I ask him, again, this time peeved, "Why am I on this boat?"

Waves still splashing against the window, he turns his head away and stares at the ocean.

I raise my voice and ask one last question: "What is Carmine Island?"

He is taking no notice of me, staring at the ocean with his vacant, dark, deep eyes.

'The Golden Leaves'

The afternoon sun still bright in the sky, the warm rays hitting my eyes and blocking the view of my mother waving on the side of the railway tracks. The grass illuminated with iridescent green, the branches of passing trees swaying forwards and backwards with the wind, her waving arm slowly disappearing, sun rays fully blinding my vision.

I squint my watery eyes, taking one last, long breath of freshly-cut grass through the sunlit train window. As the train speeds, heading south, the rolling hills take in the striking colours of the expansive landscape. Yellow and orange hues melting into serene blue, I watch the transforming sky with my face almost pressed to the window glass.

My moment of serenity is suddenly shattered by cacophony from the train tracks. I am trying to keep my balance but the vibration from the railway bridge is throwing me back and forth.

The train is gently hissing away again, and I head towards my carriage. I glance at my ticket number and find my seat at the end of the quiet carriage. I'm hoping not to interrupt an elderly lady peacefully knitting away in the window seat, the needles steadily clicking against each other. I put my luggage away and quietly sit next to her, straightening my legs. Her aging face makes me think about my grandparents and my dwelling emotions turn into a darker blue hue in harmony with the sky outside. I remember the time when I peeked around grandfather's wheelchair shouting "Peek-a- Boo!" but he didn't budge. As a child, I couldn't understand why he had sunken into grimness and kept bugging Grandmother for answers. As she slowly creaked back and forth in her rocking chair, watching over Grandfather, she stated: "Sadness is a key to true happiness. This is why the men fought in the war, for us to be happy and free. Without sadness and suffering, we would never have been free and happy. He is quiet now, so that you can play around and laugh."

Her calm voice still echoing in my ears, the passing trees sway in the wind as the heaviness in my chest starts to disappear. Everything becomes peaceful.

A large, silver knitting needle rolls on the floor and stops near the tip of my shoe. I'm about to pick it up when the lady's shapely eyebrows lead me to stare at her aging face, and her emerald green eyes look up with a friendly smile. As she picks up the needle, our knees brush and she asks, "So where are you heading, little cat?" she leans closer, jabbing her finger in her face.

"To the city, to start my studies," I say a little sheepishly.

"Brave little cat you are!" her lips curling upwards, she turns back to her knitting.

The soothing sound of the train makes me sleepy. I take a bite of the apple my mother gave me at the station. As the city slowly glides into view, my apple falls from my sleepy hands, rolling down the train corridor.

Stretching my weightless arms up and arching my back like a Cheshire cat, I wrench myself awake.

The train hisses to a halt and the elderly lady is already on her unsteady legs, pushing past with her handbags and various plastic bags with knitting items.

"Ouch! That hurt!" I hold my arm as her needle scrapes through a layer of my skin.

"Sorry, little cat. I didn't mean to stitch you!" She abruptly pushes her way through the carriage, other passengers raising their arms so that she doesn't stitch them up too.

How did she strip back that conditioned layer of friendly manner and smiles out of the blue? Are people not intrinsically who they appear to be? I gasp quietly as I touch my tingling skin, feeling taken aback. I stare at her as she picks my apple up off the floor with her chewed fingernails, shamelessly wiping it on her flowery dress and splattering saliva as she loudly bites away, wiping her mouth on a sleeve.

"At least it's not bleeding!" a passenger pushing past motions towards my arm.

I stand on the windy platform. The other passengers have disembarked and disappeared, exiting to all different directions, wheeling mounds of luggage behind them.

"Oh no! Shoot me!" Cold blood pounds in the back of my head, my hands trembling. I start rummaging through my suitcase; "My address book!"

An unsettling feeling grabs me by the throat. The darkness is slowly falling, and the lights on the platform turn on as my rapid breathing turns into white puffs in the crisp air. I start frantically pulling everything out of the suitcase with sweaty palms, my heart pounding.

"I can't have left it behind!" I bite my lip as I pull out a thick black jumper and swing it in the air. As the address book hits the pavement, my heart thumps so loudly I am lucky the platform is empty. Paging through the centre section of the book, I find the college address and wheel the suitcase out of the platform across the bustling train station. Large advertising billboards overwhelm me; the bold, highly contrasting colours selling illusions, making big impacts on your emotions. I can't locate the maps.

"Familiar face!" I recognise the tall man standing straight, adjusting his wrist watch near a vending machine.

Biting my red, swollen lip, I approach him and stand directly in front of him as he continuously taps on the glass of his watch.

"Excuse me, I need to get to the College Campus. We were on the same train..." I say with a fading voice like a little mouse, twitching my fingers nervously.

The conductor of the train slowly looks up.

"I need to find the city maps," I add, raising my voice a little, my mind going berserk. Without saying a word, he slowly motions to the left of the train terminal. I thank him, but he has already returned his gaze to his watch.

I rush through the bustling station, abruptly stumbling over someone wheeling an oversized suitcase in front of me. I get up, blushing, and apologise quietly.

'Watch where you're going, idiot!" the angry voice echoes across the cold station and, startled, I take a step back.

Walking towards the maps, wheeling my suitcase, my mind wanders back home. Moonlight shining through the window by the sink in our small galley kitchen, the sound of Mother pouring evening tea into white and pink china cups, her presence peaceful and safe.

Walking slowly, I glance at the large walls, echoing all the hustle and bustle, making me feel cornered and trapped. A rush of helplessness rushes through me, stronger than before. The colours of the imaginative train map flicker and flash in front of me as I struggle to breathe.

The next morning as I look through a sunlit window, I admire how I made it through the first night of my new journey. With my beaming smile, I watch the colours of the autumn leaves making their home on the ground, making the world appear warm and golden.

I watch the students make their way across the courtyard, some playfully kicking and scattering the leaves everywhere. I hear laugher from the distance, and I no longer feel petrified of the world.

More than twenty years later, I sit down on the front steps of our house waiting for my daughter. I watch her drag her over-packed bags, ready to burst as much as she is, with excitement. She's ready to join the race, just like I did. I remember the day I joined the other students, but never wasted a single second running any race other than my own. I had hopes and goals, like everyone else, and we were all going to get medals at the end of it. I learned to take one for the team, explore tolerance and compassion, but as we grew and ran our races in life, we ended up with self-imposed protective security walls, scared of it all unravelling around us like a loose thread on a jumper. There are no walls around my daughter, as she jumps in the car with her crisp white t-shirt on, the golden writing shining in the sun, reading *"Good vibes only!"*

As we drive towards the station, I begin to tell her my story of leaving home, the warm fuzzy feeling of nostalgia running through me as I turn the sharp corner.

"You know, the new brings excitement and happiness, but it also brings along quite a bit of stress." Our mother and daughter conversations never required watering down, but I'm not sure what to tell her now. "I'm glad you decided to go. Within a short time, you'll realise you have already learned and experienced more than you ever imagined. There's competitiveness, but don't ever let that dig down into what it is you are here to deliver to the world."

She stares at her phone, chewing gum, and slowly nods.

As I hear her mobile phone beeping and vibrating, I wonder if the pressure of the modern world is more intense than it was for me all those years ago, but how would I know? What I know from experience is that the pressure mounting on you can make it all even more exciting. It forces you to leave your mother's cosy white-washed kitchen, and when you look back to the beginning of your journey, you know you left a piece of you behind. It's hard to think about it all without bittersweet emotions, a smile escaping from my lips, the salty tears filling up my eyes.

I continue to talk, as I manoeuvre through the afternoon traffic: "I have been really thinking about this the last couple of weeks, and getting a bit upset, but I think it's me who is getting more vulnerable here. I knew you were leaving and I've been like a pressure cooker, busting for a release of tears and emotion. Sorry if I embarrass you and cry at the station…"

My daughter's laughter overpowers me. Her phone beeps and she keeps swiping and scrolling the screen with laugher. My eyes focus on her happiness. I stay quiet.

As we approach the train station, I wish she could have stayed longer with me, and I will always have that wish as a parent. For the shortest seconds of my life, I hold her close. "Mum! I got to go!" she smiles and pushes away.

I hear the train call out the last passengers and she runs through a perfectly bunched pile of autumn leaves. The heaviness in my chest grows to a squeezing sensation, my muscles tense up. The golden leaves scatter everywhere.

I see a man standing tall with his back to me, waving at someone leaving. I hear high heels clicking on the concrete pavement behind me. As I quickly glance, my eyes are met with the teary eyes of two women waving. A man walks next to me, his eyes fixated on the leaving train. We are all waving in beautiful harmony, and I can almost hear the joint drumming of our fast-beating hearts.

Walking back to the car, I glance over my shoulder and see a man sweeping all the golden leaves into a perfect pile. I conjure the magic of days gone by, and that little beacon of light inside me that kept me going. My mind filled with memories, I almost miss the faint beep of my phone in my purse. My watery eyes light up as I read the message;

"Mum, just found my seat. I left you something on the kitchen table, I hope you like it! Talk later, love you."

Arriving home, I see a white t-shirt on the kitchen table. I straighten it out and smile. The golden writing in a modern, cursive, feminine font reads *"Good vibes only!"* and just like that, she turns me into the person I am supposed to be, the mother who has the daughter who is exactly the person she is supposed to be. As we get older we may not need to see new landscapes, but we may need new eyes to see what we have already seen.

Symbolism mythology, cultural background and childhood memories

As we write, we can introduce symbols into our narratives. I was able to tap into painful areas such as feelings of sorrow and emptiness without the narrative sounding too shallow by simply adding symbolism to the content.

I started my novel by writing a scene in the ocean. The ocean has the symbolic meaning of a source of life, death, chaos, and even collective unconsciousness.

I moved on to the sky, as the protagonists were travelling by plane. The sky can mean fate or heaven. It was essentially a fish out of water story, so the fate was already set out for the main character. Next, I had fire set up in the story. Fire has a meaning of hell, life or lust. It is also our inner light, determination and passion. The protagonist ends up digging up soil and the soil becomes somewhat the core of the story. Soil means abundance and fertility.

I also threw in snakes, and this reminded me of being a little girl on the island of Crete in Greece. I bought a beautiful silver snake ring. Unfortunately, over the years, I lost it, but I remember wearing the ring and being reminded of the mythological story told by the Greeks. I also added a snake in the chapter where my protagonist visits India. Here we see a different symbolic take on the snake with the God Shiva. The snake around her neck represents toxic communication. This metaphor fitted perfectly with my novel's narrative.

In the below samples, the snake slithers through into the house of an evil woman as a warning for her to stop doing bad things and in 'India,' the snake is used in its cultural context.

Symbol: Snakes

'A Warning'

The warning comes out of the blue.

At Carol's filthy farm, the snakes keep swarming towards the house, hissing in the dark of the night, their two-pronged tongues flickering in and out. The clever king snake moves unnoticed, even though he is big enough to suck the life out of a human.

Carol is sitting at her computer, typing her daily self-appraisal, boasting about her accomplishments on Facebook, displaying her narcissistic trait. She's left the door ajar. Who would willingly walk into that house anyway? Carol is sniffling loudly through her congested nose, coughing and spitting up grey phlegm on the walls. The house is cold, the wallpaper ripped and the white paint underneath chipped. Maybe the phlegm keeps the wallpaper intact. The king snake begins to crawl up Carol's leg. It all happens in seconds.

The snake gives her a quick bite and moves so quickly down her leg she has no time to react. When she does, the quick snake is already out of the door.

Carol's eyes bulge out as she screams in pain. She grabs the nearest thing, a mop standing in a large bucket of dirty water against the wall. Bucket upside down, water everywhere, she is holding the mop and slipping across the floor, swearing. No point; the snake is already outside in the safety of the long, green grass.

Carol is fuming outside, aimlessly hitting the grass with the mop.

She goes back in the house, pulls over a plastic chair and sits with her knees touching.

Her left leg has a tiny little hole in it, no blood.

Later that night, a sharp headache hits her. She feels exhausted. She is not one to go to the doctor, because doctors in Garmsby cost money.

Next day, both exhaustion and headaches continue. She is swearing and hitting her animals with sticks with the little energy she has left. She locks malnourished birds in their cages and spits at them. The temperature has risen to an all-year high in Garmsby, but Carol is not concerned about giving the animals any extra water. She was born to torture both animals and people.

She slams the barn door, goes back inside the house whilst sniffling, sucking and spitting, through her sinuses to the back of her throat, up in her mouth, then out on the nearest wall. In the daylight, the wallpaper gleams with phlegm.

By now, she feels so unwell she leaves the door wide open and collapses on her untidy bed. Her left leg gives out, her tongue and lips tingle and she cannot get any words out. She suffers a stroke in silence, leaving her left side virtually paralysed, depriving her of speech. She is in and out of consciousness. She's seeing great masses of snakes crawling over her body.

The stroke leaves her with some permanent damage, her speech is still gibberish and the left side of her face is droopy and weak. Little does she know that snakes have a close telepathic bond with spell rituals and are masters of slithering through.

'India'

Arriving at the hotel, my eyes instantly fixate on the large purple poster above the receptionist. The receptionist smiles at me as I greet her.

"What is the meaning of this?" I point at the poster of Shiva wearing a snake as a garland and drinking from a cup.

"Aaahh God Shiva!" she turns around and has a quick glance at the poster.

"See the snake? And the cup?"

I nod.

"The snake around her neck symbolises toxic speech, causing suffering and pain. She drinks the poison in the cup to prevent these things. Good Shiva," she smiles again and hands me the key.

Symbol: Colours

The below poem is about a woman and homelessness. I have chosen the colour grey to symbolise the world of homeless people, the streets and the general environment they live in. Grey is an emotionless, moody colour that is typically associated with the dull, dirty and dingy. It can signify loss or depression. However, it is also a timeless and practical colour signifying maturity and responsibility, often associated with old age and experience. Grey is an intermediate colour between black and white. It is a neutral or achromatic colour, meaning literally that it is a colour "without colour." It is the colour of a cloud-covered sky, of ash and of lead.

'Grey'

"Walking aimlessly, with no illusions of this world being a gem, kissing her neck and handing her a cheque, dwelling on the past in a world that is cold and hellish, she still thought she had lived wisely and well. Facing the darkness falling upon her like a fog rolling in off the bay, she finally agreed this is her way, in the world that is nothing but grey.
  Body shaking with fatigue and pain, her ordinary self never glowing again.
  Shaggy hair that was darker every day, clothes ripped, three more steps and she's reached the day. Losing time, closing her eyes, she spirals across the road on your way.
  Nature of life, at the end of her days, branches tweaking, snowflakes melting, dirt, rock and branches feeling like home again, she is pleading her exquisite anger away.
  If you ignore her hunching in pain, the streets will remain, forever, glowing in grey."

Symbol: Night

Night can be used in connection to darkness, acts as a cover over the world and can be used to represent the 'end of the road.' It can symbolise peace or tranquillity or death and darkness, concerning the usage of shadows. The great thing about night is that, if the writer takes time to mention the moon, stars, comets, asteroids, meteors, lamp posts, any type of light, the writer is trying to tell you something about the character.

There are two sides; night is the end of the day, where things are hidden in shadows, but if there is a source of light, even a small one, the writer is trying to tell you about some internal or external conflict. Things in the light are generally safe, but things in the dark can be susceptible to danger. Within religion, God's first act is to create light and dispel darkness. Darkness and night therefore symbolise a world without God's presence. Night always occurs when suffering is worst, and its presence in the bible reflects Eliezer's belief that he lives in a world without God. 'Meeting at Night' is a Victorian English love poem by Robert Browning, (1845). This poem is a great example of the use of a symbol. The entire poem has a sense of movement to it that reflects the writer's desire to reunite with his love. The poem's rhythm clearly denotes a sense of pressing intent, however the poem abruptly ends as he meets his love. We could assume that once he has attained his happiness, there is no need to write more about it.

There is a touch of secrecy in the poem; the journey and reunion happen at night, suggesting a veil of transgression that, in the Victorian age, would likely be linked to sexuality and secrets.

Here is an example of how I added 'night' into my novel:

The intense light shines through my eyes as I take the plunge down, every ripple of the blood adds to the beauty, the serenity of the night sky. As I flee to the night, I finally feel complete. If you knew me yesterday, you don't know me anymore.

Cultural background:

We will never know all the reasons why we are who we are and we don't have the power to choose where we come from or our cultural background, but we can choose where we go from there and how we use our own culture.

After reviewing some of my creative writing, even without intention, my own cultural background was evident from my stories.

When working on my first novel, I intentionally looked into history, climate and ancient cultural practices and placed them all into the storyline. Here is a sample of how this was incorporated into a story directly, turning this chapter into a mythic tale:

'Witches Drum'

Grandmother Eva was old, frail and spoke a lot of stuff that made no sense to me, but she was an amazing cook and from then on, I grew up hanging from her apron strings. I learned more from her than at the St Petersburg boarding school.

My mother once told me a story about her and I am sure she left many things out of it as she thought I was too young to understand.

Grandmother had been born all the way up past the Arctic Circle, in the tundra, among the Saami people, including the Lapland witches who could curse people. She lived her childhood through harsh but magical winters and hot, white summer nights full of snakes and mosquitoes, learning about nature and our connection with the universe. Later, she had fallen in love with a soldier, who had been taken as a prisoner of war and sent to a labour camp in Siberia. She was warned that it was most likely he had already died due to the harsh camp conditions and long hours of exhausting physical work, but instead, she firmly believed her Saami people had cursed him.

After the war, she left her family far away in Lapland. Against all the advice and warnings from the village elders, she somehow managed to cross the border to the Soviet Union, armed only with her determination and a Saami witches drum. She planned to use the drum to undo the curse set by her very own people, but to do this, she had to find her beloved soldier.

The trip across the border through strange places and hurdles lasted weeks, but she had spirit, gained from being born at the tundra, with its painstakingly cold winds that hurt even the strongest and thickest bones.

She managed to get as far as the trans-Siberian railway. On the train, she finally relaxed and sighed with satisfaction, but exhausted both physically and emotionally, she fell asleep.

She woke up to find out that not only she, but all the other passengers too, had been robbed. It looked like a professional robbery, orchestrated by the Russian mafia; the passengers of two full carriages all robbed blind. She lost her identity papers, some money and her most prized-possession; the witches drum. The drum was indigenous handcraft, with beautifully carved shaman symbols showing the three worlds; underworld, middle (human) world and upper world, covered by real, soft, reindeer skin.

Without identity papers, she was removed from the train and returned to St Petersburg, but refused to board the ship heading back to her homeland without her brave soldier. She believed one day he would be back alive and well from Siberia.

This never happened. The anger and frustration over the consequences of the long, painful war left her searching for the small, peculiar drum and having strong doubts over her own people.

She never found the original one taken from her in the train robbery, even though she was crazy enough to go back to Moscow, to go searching among the hardest of the criminals in the dark and run-down Moscow suburbs; the suburbs that only the bravest of men would willingly enter, let alone a woman from a different country. One of the Mafia men felt sorry for her and directed her to a wood carver in St Petersburg for a new drum, all paid for. This man walked her to the train station, bought her a one-way ticket and handed her a piece of paper with a name and a street address. He watched the train leave from afar and made sure no one stepped out of her carriage.

She was on her way back to St Petersburg, once again, whether she liked it or not, holding an address for her next mission. Within days, she had a new drum made for her by a handsome Ukrainian wood carver, Victor. Victor was very talented and carved her one out of beautiful solid pinewood. Not only was Victor talented, but he was also very charming and handsome. She carefully instructed him to hand-paint the right shamanic symbols with proper ink and she was over the moon to be able to call the spirits again and undo the curse she still believed was placed upon her soldier. This somewhat made her feel alive again.

Grandmother fell in love again and, surprisingly, settled in St Petersburg.

She ended up having my mother in St Petersburg and lived her life as a dutiful parent until my mother was old enough to attend boarding school.

Victor had more work in Moscow and Eva left with him. She was happy to leave St Petersburg and my mother believed she found it too hard to live there, near the harbour, seeing the ships leave every day.

During all those years in the Soviet Union, the relatives of Eva were desperate to get her back to Lapland, to the Arctic Circle, but she refused. She allowed them, however, to pay for my mother's schooling and that was the compromise in their lives. My mother had loved St Petersburg, beautiful parklands and nature, but for me, it was time to say goodbye to this city, just like Grandmother Eva had done decades earlier.

I sat next to Grandmother on the packed Nikolaevsky Express train, feeling like I could weep my heart out any minute.

She gently touched my leg and said, "There will be a future, now let's go and see what kind of future it is." I smiled back at her and tried to think about the anticipation of approaching the bright lights of Moscow and if Grandmother had inherited some of those Lapland witches' genes of clairvoyance, she might set me on the right track with my life.

The train moved on fast, leaving behind the nature of St Petersburg suburbs, the magnificent, broad arrow of scenery that I was used to, for the empty, cold and strange landscape of the Moscow area.

I closed my eyes and saw the drum spinning, a warm sensation running through my body.

The magic of the drum was real, colours and images flashing in front of me, the witches whispering secrets in my ears. They didn't sound like fearsome goddesses of witchcraft, but certainly capable of jinx, if necessary.

I took one deep breath and opened my eyes. The train kept moving at a steady speed, leaving behind a white cloud of fog, lingering, like the voices of the witches in my ear.

Childhood memories:

Writing happy childhood memories is a big part of my recovery and it helps stop them from fading away. Sensory details and lessons learned are some examples of showing memory in a context.

'On the warm tin roof'

The beauty of the morning light is shining through the window, vivid memories of the blissful days at Grandmother's house filling my quiet mind. I can't lift myself up. I'm bedridden now.

I swipe the grey hairs off my forehead and smile at the window, closing my eyes.

I'm slowly falling into my own hypnosis, consciously remembering every detail of that mystical day.

My smile widening, the vibrational energy is bringing me joy, ecstasy, happiness and peace. I remember my Spirit, as the Spiritual Source beams through me.

I am climbing up on the tin roof, the sun is shining bright and starting to burn the bottom of my feet. I tiptoe further up and decide to lie down. The tin roof warms my back and my green summer dress floats in the gentle wind. I pull a white fresh flower out of my pocket. I place it near my nostrils and smell the earthy scent. I pick off white petals, one by one, slowly, leaving the yellow middle part staring at me. I throw it by my side and cross my arms on top of myself. Clouds, puffy cotton balls floating in the huge azure sky, like a happy dance, the big bright sun following them. I can stay on the roof all day if I like. It's so peaceful I close my eyes and dream.

Lying on that tin roof, I feel pure and complete bliss. Simple happiness, only created by the sunlight, the flower and the passing clouds.

I don't want this to end. Ever.

Someone is gently shaking me. My old bones almost rattle. I open my eyes and see Nurse's white uniform. I can see her mouth moving but I can't hear her. She brings in a tray full of medicine and needles. I gasp.

On the day I'm leaving this earth, my Spirit came back to me, from a long, long time ago.

I touch Nurse's arm with my cold hand, and for the last time, I take in a deep breath before returning to my warm tin roof.

Lifestyle writing

Lifestyle writing is one of the easiest ways to start writing. You can find a wide variety of ideas from everyday life. It's likely that the subject you are writing about has been covered before, but this doesn't matter; you just need to write it from your own unique point of view.

'How to Live With Integrity (And Find Your Purpose along the Way)'

Most parents teach their children that you need to respect yourself by living in a manner that is consistent with your purpose, values, and personal goals. When you live with integrity, you set a positive example. Dealing with groups of children and teenagers, we encounter all the stereotypes: the kids who bully, the kids who sit on the sidelines, the gossipers, kids who take charge, and kids who are victimized. We encounter parents who have developed either negative or positive habits and push these habits onto their children.

We may not all be able to get along due to the different values and habits, but how can we live with more integrity despite our backgrounds and beliefs?

1. Identify your habits

We all do certain things a certain way every single day — the way you tie your shoelaces, the way you greet or acknowledge your neighbour or mailman, the way you like your coffee or play with your hair. Some of our bad decisions are down to force of habit and become second nature to us. Maybe you are always avoiding confrontation and people due to past experiences, or you are always late, or you fail to respond to emails or calls, or you spend too much time on social media, or you overspend your money. We sometimes fail to see our negative behaviour patterns and the way they might affect other people.

To be able to live with more integrity is to identify these patterns, recognize that they might be a problem for others, and aim to replace them with positive habits. Acknowledge your neighbour by saying hello, answer your phone, spend less time on social media, and give more attention to other things around you. You can even compliment a stranger daily and see the smile on their face to step into a more positive behaviour pattern.

2. Accept that we all make wrong choices sometimes

If you recognize negative habits that have affected other people around you, accept what happened and learn from it to make smarter decisions in the future. Don't be too hard on yourself, and remind yourself that we all make mistakes at some point in our lives. Sometimes these mistakes guide us to see our vision for life clearer and eventually fulfill our purpose. Nothing in life is constantly perfect — we are always evolving and learning.

3. See each relationship as bidirectional

In our relationships, it is essential to have mutual trust and respect. This is not always easy, especially among children and teenagers who are all still figuring out how to build supportive relationships. Oftentimes, adults still haven't learned how to be consistent with their values. It is important to make effective decisions in regards to helping others, as this adds value to your own life. When you listen to someone and give them a little bit of your time, you will encourage feelings of trust and compassion to your own life.

4. When you start believing in yourself, others will follow your example

You set yourself up to become successful in life only when you believe in yourself. Only then can you inspire and motivate others with your actions. Setting a positive example is not always smooth sailing, especially if you are up against complicated matters and people with conflicts.

The way to influence positively is to stick to your words and get things done by holding on to your positive habits, values, purpose, and goals. If someone doesn't respect your values, it may be impossible to stride towards a healthy relationship. They might be even emotionally harming you with their anger which is toxic. We can sometimes try to hold space for anger if it's a conscious expression of one's feelings and unmet needs, but not when it's holding blame or insults. We need to respect ourselves enough to be able to move on with integrity.

Always aim to keep your circle positive, as life is way too short for constantly dealing with negativity. When you learn to make effective decisions, you see the difference in positivity around you. We are all in a journey of evolution we don't plan.

"Who am I?" and "What's my purpose?" are two simple fundamental questions we need to remind ourselves of when we are feeling lost and need to get back on track with living with our best life.

'5 Ways to Use the Law of Attraction to Improve Your Life'

1. Stay positive and thankful

The Law of Attraction is all about you attract what you are sending out, therefore it is important to stay positive. If you are feeling negative vibes, you're sending out negative signals to the universe and in turn, being rewarded with more negativity. You can change your vibration from low to high by doing something that makes you feel good, even if it is for only less than an hour per day. When you start feeling more positive and thankful for everything good you can find in your life, you will be rewarded with higher vibration and positive outcomes.

2. Clear your resentment

If you feel like despite trying to manifest with positivity and thankfulness nothing is going right, you need to look deeper into your forms of resistance. You are most likely feeling frustrated, you have doubts about manifesting, you regret things you have done in your life and paths you have taken leading to anxiety. You need to clear all the resistance and sometimes you can't do this by yourself. There is nothing wrong with asking for help, whether it is from a friend, therapist or through activities.

3. Start co-creating

You need to set clear goals to be able to achieve them. If you struggle with goal setting, look for inspiration. Study the people who have already achieved what you want and ask for help from professionals. Reading books and researching is co-creating with the universe to help you figure out your ultimate goals.

4. Follow the signs

The Universe is constantly sending us signs. It is up to you to acknowledge the signs around you. Signs are personal messages directing you towards your goals and they can sometimes be unexpected.

5. Ask

Once you have worked on a positive mindset, cleared your resentments, started co-creating and followed the signs you are ready to ask the Universe what you truly desire. What you don't ask, you don't get. It is up to you how you will amplify your vibrations. You can be creative and create vision boards, draw mind maps, paint or write a letter. Or you can quietly pray and meditate. At this final stage, you need to trust the Universe is working for you.

'How to Show More Gratitude and Have a Better Life Instantly'

When children are given gifts at their birthday parties, they often get so embarrassed that they hide behind their parents or don't know where to look. We all smile at the children and know their behavior is not because they are ungrateful but because they feel overwhelmed and humbled. We also know that with time they learn to express gratitude in different ways, even if it is just quietly whispering, "Thank you."

We all show gratitude in different ways. Some of us struggle to open up and might feel like we haven't shown enough, while some of us feel just like the small children — overwhelmed and humbled by gratitude, often taken by surprise that we don't know how to accept gifts and show how grateful we really are deep down. How do we start showing more gratitude and turn our lives into a positive chain of events instantly?

You can start by listing five to 10 things you are grateful for at this moment. It's easier to start with thinking about all the small and free pleasures of life. This can vary from the kindness people have shown you lately to a healthy mind and body that allows you to enjoy life. Be grateful for the awareness of having all the people and things in your life, your strength, and courage to complete daily responsibilities.

As you immerse yourself in what's already happened in your life and how much you have, you can move on to what's to come. Being grateful in advance for the abundance that's on the way — it's as important as the present and past.

You can start feeling gratefulness towards your future — new opportunities, career prospects, a network of friends or travel. And while you are thinking about your list, don't forget to tap into the most powerful source you have access to, the source that is responsible for where you are right now and where you are supposed to be going: your imagination. Once you feel the gratitude and have a concentrated intention, you can start expressing it. You can start this by thanking the kind people you listed before. Send them a thank you note, do them a favor or acknowledge them publicly. Thankfulness implies an outward expression of one's gratitude.

Benefits of making gratitude a daily habit include a positive attitude and less judgment. One great daily habit of showing gratitude is being an active listener. Acknowledge the speaker with your body language and encourage positive feedback. Making good eye contact is a great daily habit that shows gratitude and shows that you are focused and paying attention.

You don't have to be giving out daily over-the-top compliments to show gratitude. Just being there and being thoughtful is oftentimes enough. Volunteer in your community and share your skills, but do everything with a positive attitude and smile often. A simple smile from you can instantly brighten up someone's day. With a little practice, your abilities to show gratitude will come to you naturally and open your life up to receiving more abundance leading to a better life.

Trust in your heart, your soul, your mind, and body that you are a grateful person who is at peace with expressing your feelings of gratitude beyond the child who is too overwhelmed and humbled.

'Need guidance? Stop asking for it and you'll find it!'

This year, for me, started with a feeling of severe desperation. The previous year had been full of small, medium and large failures in every aspect of my life. I failed friendships, I didn't get jobs I applied for, I dedicated myself to writing a novel that no one was interested in, I was diagnosed with a couple of severe health issues and I was hurt by those closest to me, to the point of tears and loss of contact. I felt like a thorough failure, and slowly started to believe that maybe the world was better off without me. Everything felt dreadful. I put on an act of normality to fool everyone that I was ok.

Suddenly it was the end of January and I had already finished all the new releases in the self-help section of my local library.

My bedroom floor was also covered in the old self-help books I was re-reading, highlighting quotes and marking important chapters that I felt gave me some sort of guidance in life. I felt utterly desperate, there was no doubt about it, and no matter how aggressively I re-read the likes of Tony Robbins, there was no hope in sight. Maybe I just couldn't break the barriers between theory and practice. I felt like Emma Thompson's character in 'Love Actually,' having to go out and be cheerful, when I was distraught. Emma Thompson's character realises her partner is cheating, sobbing and biting her lip. That was me every day, except I had been cheated on by life. Everything that it promised, all the hopes and dreams, were dangled in front of me like a carrot, then taken away. I started to pile up the old books and one caught my eye among the self-help titles; 'The Alchemist' by Paulo Coelho. My chest heaving in desperation, I picked up the novel and asked the universe to give me a sign from it. If this novel is all about omens and going in circles trying to find the meaning of life, maybe there was a key word inside the book for me to discover? I blindly pinpointed my finger to the sentence: *"because they don't follow their hearts."*

Had I been living my life all wrong?

I had been asking for signs, omens, anything to drop out of the sky, but I forgot about looking inside my own inner guidance system. From then on, I promised myself I would stop searching for omens that mean nothing. I was going to aim for a mental state of 'being in a flow' trying to enjoy and focus, not only with my writing but life itself too. Only a few months later, knowing that I am allowed to follow my intuition from the bottom of my heart, I can just relax into life.

I don't need to look for feathers falling out of the sky or search for interpretations of everything online; the architectural canvas of life is right in front of us. We only see tiny parts of it, but that's how it's meant to be, that is life, and if you are not relaxed into your own life, then what is the point? It was a wake-up call for me to stop searching and wasting time fighting to see into the future. When we want to see the future, the signs and omens, what we are really doing is controlling and trying to force life to go our way. What the random pin-point sentence of 'The Alchemist' taught me is that you need to become friends with your heart, but to be able to apply this, you also need to do full-circle searching; only then will you realise that the answer was within yourself all along.

Life is never easy, not even when you find your flow. We can't control everything in life anyway, and sometimes no matter how much we work towards something, it isn't meant for us. I have stopped beating myself up about things I have no control over and started trusting my inner guidance system. I don't see the entire architectural canvas of life. I am only meant to see what I see, and follow the little pieces thrown into my life, both good and bad. I look back at all the 'dreadful' pieces of life thrown at me last year, and wonder, was it really all that bad? Hardship is a sign itself. It is a sign to move away from these issues and people. Living in a flow is living in the now. This beautiful quote from Eckhart Tolle sums it up perfectly: **"As soon as you honour the present moment, all unhappiness and struggle dissolve, and life begins to flow with joy and ease. When you act out the present-moment awareness, whatever you do becomes imbued with a sense of quality, care and love—even the most simple action."**

I thought about how I, at a young age, was introduced to the spiritual world by my grandmother, and this led me to be deeply interested in existential questions, which later led to interest in personal development. No matter how much I read and related my knowledge, I couldn't apply any of it. I made it too complicated in my understanding and kept searching for something that was as bizarre as my grandmother's made-up spiritual teachings. All I had to apply was the knowledge of myself. I see now that I was being impatient and demanding. I am not weak, I am not a failure and tomorrow is a fresh opportunity to just go with the flow with all the blood my heart is pumping.

'Turning Point'

When I paint, the visual world is absorbed into the canvas like smoke, where it will reform, whole and alive, fully adapted to its new environment. This is my 'Turning Point' for anxiety and post-traumatic stress disorder due to severe cyber bullying, lasting eight long years. I sought help. Saw doctors. Learned coping techniques. I tried therapy, meditation and even medication. Being a victim of bullying isn't new or unique, millions of people suffer physical and verbal abuse every single day, but the not-so brave world of social media has exacerbated it; the damage people can do is wider and the relentless online bullies are always ready to torment other victims. Bullying has a profound effect on all aspects of a person's health as well as their work and family life. Its knock-on effect on the community and economy is huge, and like a noxious weed, bullies find a way, another app, another social media account, to carry on. There are so many different forms of cyber bullying: exclusion, harassment, outing, publicly humiliating, cyberstalking, flaming (bullying tactic using online arguments), dissing (posting screenshots, damaging photos), trickery (gaining trust and then sending private information to others), trolling (insulting, personally attacking to provoke response) and catfishing (creating fake social networking profiles). All these forms of bullying should elicit a response, not from the victim, but others around, identifying the bullying. The emergence of the bullying should coincide with an active response, clearly signalling how wrong it is, and as soon as the bullying starts, so should the response of not tolerating the bad behaviour. However, what I learned was that we often continue to use the technique of being nice or ignoring it, leading to unresolved prolonged conflict. I discovered the terrifying truth; bullies do not hold the same beliefs, there are no apologies or compassion, instead the bullies see you as a soft target and will keep on going until they break you. This is exactly what they find satisfying, seeing you suffer and fall, whilst they are feeding their own disillusioned egos. Eventually bullying starts preventing you doing things the way you should. The scale of devastation bullying had on me made me realise that I can no longer tolerate cyber bullying, in any form, or from anyone. I lost the career that I had worked for all my life, ending up long-term unemployed and scared to have social media access. I isolated myself, which also leads to loss of important friendships. Emotional pain can't directly kill you, but running from it can. Bullying causes us, the victims, to hide behind a veil, and fail by default. It leaves deep scars, and recovery is a difficult, long road. In the aftermath, whilst we are trying to protect ourselves, we also stop living. I stopped living for years, pulling the blanket over me and staying in bed. I'll never get those years back. To survive the severe intimidation and public humiliation of cyber bullying is nothing short of a miracle. Bullies are desperate to kill your kindness, to get a negative reaction out of you and make you sink to their level, but when you come out of the traumatic experience with compassion and kindness, *they* ultimately fail.

Creative arts and painting made me leave the feelings of anger and hatred behind and re-discover the authentic self again. When I picked up my paint brush, I seemed more relaxed and less edgy. Discovering art and painting was a turning point, from victim to resilient self, and I slowly started to defend my life again. I was able to express the emotional pain I had felt for so long in a non-judgemental environment. It was a deeply satisfying feeling, and I felt emotionally stronger.

When I believed I was finally starting to reach out to better days, a ghastly panic washed over me like a cold sea wave. I felt physically sick, every part of my body going cold and still. The bullies, who tormented me for eight long years, were suddenly posting anti-bullying campaigns, trying to progress their own agenda. I knew that they were nothing but narcissists fuelling their beliefs of their self-importance and superiority, trying to gain attention and admiration, and worst of all, pretending to be victims in order to manipulate others. Bullies always speak for attention. They need to validate themselves, justifying and adding value to their delusional lives.

It would have been so easy to fall into the 'life is so unfair' negativity, but exceptional life involves challenges, and fairness is relative. Instead of crawling back to my bed and underneath the covers, feeling the world's darkness all around me like I always used to with these kinds of setbacks, I decided to pick up the paint brush. I reminded myself to re-focus from others to myself, to not allow them, ever again, to have tremendous power over my wellbeing. I made the decision to focus on better things and take responsibility for my own feelings. I was the one holding resentment, feeling angry and allowing them, eight years on, to make me feel miserable. I had to get better at shifting my perspective and reframing the negatives quickly, knowing that I am stronger than that. I reminded myself that we live in an unlimited, expanding universe. In order for us to exist in this universe, we must expand with it. Elie Wiesel, a Holocaust survivor, once said that "Our obligation is to give meaning to life, and in doing so to overcome the passive, indifferent life." The bullies had been working hard for eight years to give me the passive life, whilst they were taking on the active, meaningful life, even with their lies and bad behaviour. I was never going to have a meaningful life, expanding with the universe, inspiring and empowering people around me, feeling like this. That was the moment I made the decision to move on, and even if the same bullies returned in the future, I would look away, for good, with the help of my creative mind, paint brushes and knowing that the unlimited universe had my back, even if no one else had.

Ready to unleash your writing to the world?

If you have reached the point where you are ready for your writing to see daylight, you may want to consider sending it to traditional publishers, or self-publish. Traditional publishers pay for your manuscript and may give you an advance, but to get there, you may need to find a literary agent. In general, traditional publishers will help you with editing, printing and marketing, but because they carry the cost of all this, you as an author may end up with less money in your pocket, compared to self-publishing. Self-publishing means you are doing it yourself. All of it. With self-publishing, you not only need to consider quality and getting it into bookstores, but how you are going to sell your work. You will also need to write down lists of ways to promote your work, such as traditional book launches, tours and book signings, online marketing campaigns; heavy social media presence with feedback and the option to engage, book trailers, video testimonials on YouTube and Instagram, press releases for PR Web and translating the book to increase the sales reach. You may need to create a movement around the book along the lines of: What's your story — is it your personal story? Maybe you're battling similar issues? Or maybe you can be the voice of a group? Help bring people together or get attention for those who may get ignored or marginalised in society. You also need to consider all aspects of your target market. Practise describing your target market, going beyond sentences such as, *"Women purchase the majority of books and I expect the readership for this novel to be 60% female and*

aged between 17 and 40" by evaluating and researching your potential market. It may be a niche market that you are looking at, but once you have done your research, you may find that even niche markets may have thousands of potential readers.

A book blurb acts as a short sales pitch for your work. A synopsis is an overview of your entire work, which needs to include the plot. Practise writing both of these and remember that they are generally written in the present tense.

As an example, I have used a fictional novel, "Otherness".

Example of book blurb:

'Otherness'

"Evelyn. Get a human skull. Make sure you clean the bones, maceration is important. Soften the solid by soaking as I instructed. Then it is your time to create something important. Remember, we spoke about the creative process giving life a meaning and the keenest pleasures are not always moral?"
Dr Odugo, Bening City Edo, Nigeria.
Her only hope lies with her own secret past.
In a leafy suburb of St Petersburg, Russian Evelyn Nazarenko endures tragic circumstances early in her life. She copes by writing stories about escaping from humanity, into the world of the undead.

One day, it all changes when a charming and grand man walks into her life. Completely taken by the sudden whirlwind romance, Evelyn comes out of her shell and the man whisks her off to a faraway land, Australia. Evelyn, naively expects a trouble-free lifestyle with constant sunshine and glamorous beaches, but the companionship she was hoping for turns into loneliness, and she returns to her world of the undead.

On a weekend trip, overhearing a shocking discovery, everything changes for the worst. She can't watch from afar and live in the knowledge of evil, but by pursuing this, she discovers that everything in her own life has been a lie. She sees the possibility of being a vampire as a gift rather than a curse, and uses the uniqueness for the benefit of herself and others, but can she discover the truth by saving herself and those she cares about before it's too late?

Example of synopsis:

'Otherness'

"Evelyn. Get a human skull. Make sure you clean the bones, maceration is important. Soften the solid by soaking as I instructed. Then it is your time to create something important. Remember, we spoke about the creative process giving life a meaning and the keenest pleasures are not always moral?"
Dr Odugo, Bening City Edo, Nigeria.

In a leafy suburb of St Petersburg, Russian Evelyn Nazarenko endures tragic circumstances early in her life; her father's sudden death from cancer and her mother's mysterious accident that left her dying alone on a St Petersburg street one early winter's morning in 1992. All this makes Evelyn write stories in her red journal; one of them being about the mysterious Palm Island that makes her believe that she is transitioning from humanity into a vampire, although she does question the possibility of this.

Evelyn's grandmother, Eva, picks her up to move to Moscow to live with her, and the withdrawn, shy young woman keeps to herself, baking honey layer cakes in the tiny apartment, George Herbert's poems guiding her. She starts working in a café, and one day a charming and grand Australian man walks in. They strike up a friendship that blossoms into Eva's first love with the mysterious Adrian. Hired by the Russian oil company, he is on a work assignment in Moscow and regularly visits the café Evelyn works in.

Meanwhile, Grandmother Eva lives in her own world of ancient magic rituals and Evelyn can't grasp the meaning of all Eva's rituals.

Completely taken by Adrian, Evelyn comes out of her shell and he whisks her away to a faraway land, Australia. Evelyn naively expects a trouble-free lifestyle with constant sunshine and glamorous beaches, but the companionship she was hoping for turns into loneliness, until she has a daughter, Holly.

On a weekend trip, overhearing a shocking discovery, everything changes in her life in one single moment. She can't watch from afar and live in the knowledge of evil, but by pursuing this, she discovers everything in her own life has been a lie. She encounters racism, paranoia, disappearances and murder, muddy soils of centuries-old cemeteries and red, dry dusty land, but she also learns from her own background, and that Grandmother Eva was onto something important with her rituals.

Evelyn gets taken into the complex world of black magic, and her reality becomes blurred with voices and commands, whilst Adrian has been a compulsive liar involved in the world of organised crime and impersonating his identical twin brother for his own selfish needs.

Evelyn's naive blindness makes her realise that sometimes, to survive, we need to take a plunge deeper in the mud, swim in it for a while and re-appear to discover the truth and break free, just like George Herbert. She sees the possibility of being a vampire as a gift rather than a curse and uses the uniqueness for the benefit of herself and others.

With Adrian in prison, Evelyn moves to England and eventually sees the truth Grandmother Eva summoned in her rituals. Evelyn puts the truth in the bank's safety deposit box, for now.

When she finally believes that she can leave her own tragic drama behind her, she receives a blow to the head from behind, leaving her fighting for life.

She survives and carries on with the legacy of magic with her most powerful soul; the soul she could only have gained by going through the pain and finally accepting that she is something unique; neither truly living nor truly dead.

Writing competitions and scholarships

Writing competitions often give writers the challenge of crafting a story within the confines of a certain word limit. This is far more challenging than just letting a tale unspool across as many pages as it takes.

I took part in a themed fiction competition open to all female, female-identifying and non-binary writers. The theme of the competition was 'Metamorphosis.' They were looking for creative, insightful fiction up to 2,000 words.

'Metamorphosis – A Golden Leaf'

According to the internet, I should be wrapping my stomach in body wraps now, drinking magic detox tea whilst relying on supplements, getting lip fillers so that my body will seem smaller compared to my beautiful bee-stung lips and taking endless social media pictures of my ten-minute ab workouts, posing on cardio equipment.

I haven't slept properly in weeks. I'm too anxious, always over-breathing after overeating. I lie in bed with the blue light shining on my face, checking my Instagram feed, comparing calories, outfits, lip fillers, supplements and body wraps. Thoughts of relaxing in a tropical paradise wearing a Brazilian bikini, with perfect hair and full lips drum into my head. It's all about appearances.

Inside of me, I wish I was completely green, full of kale and seaweed. I wonder what to do after bingeing on food. I always give up and continue to binge for the rest of the day, put myself down and conclude that I'm a failure, ignore the factors that brought on the binge and calorie-restrict the next day to the point of having a killer migraine all day. I dose up on anti-depressants to combat the feelings of worthlessness.

In the stillness of the dull afternoon, I'm feeling like I'm fighting to reach a mountain summit, but I'm only trying to reach for my tablets in the bathroom cabinet. I fall down on the cold floor, fast; like going down a steep mountain slope, hitting my head against the wall.

I'm floating in a false bubble of hope, observing what I am doing and who I am trying to be.

Personal growth opens and closes doors. The people around me have been eclectic, from all walks of life, and now they are mainly gone, as I've shut myself in my bubble; no moments of pure happiness, no love, grace or gratitude.

I grab a razor blade. I'm breathing too much air. Ruby-red blood splashes on my cream-coloured tights. I feel the warmth on my cold skin. A minimal amount of oxygen is being delivered to my brain and my mind slowly shuts off. I drop the razor blade.

The afternoon sun shining on the bathroom tiles makes them warm to touch. I rub my weary eyes and slowly push up from the floor. Everything seems strange, like I'm viewing myself from above. My breathing slows down to calm and quiet.

I'm a girl with mid-length dusty blonde hair and large blue eyes, walking fast out of the bathroom door. In my white dress, stained with blood, I march outside.

The wind rushing over my skin, I slide down my front stairs. I wipe the blood off my arms and keep on walking, past the neighbours without saying 'hello,' over the bridge and across the creek. My eyes fix on the view as my inner voice whispers: "Let's go down to the water. I don't imagine anyone is swimming today."

I slip on the muddy soil as the leaves dangle off the trees and fall down deep in the creek. I recall my dreams of tropical getaways, staring at my reflection. Streams of water make their way down my back as my perfect body glistens in the sunlight. I whisper 'hello, perfection' to the reflection. My breathing is quiet, calm and almost unpredictable.

Silently, my reflection disappears into tiny sparkly pieces. I am drifting into the uncharted territory of sudden metamorphosis, like a birth unfolding beautifully, unaltered and completely primal. All the overpowering influences threw me out of this world deep into the mist of the white creek.

Floating on air, with euphoric awe I tell myself "Go home."

Skimming along on the wind and viewing from above, I see my neighbour's boy sweeping the ground. Strange, I feel so light. The wind gently swirls me around above the golden leaves he has bunched perfectly into a pile. Through the sunlit window, his father peers up from his crinkled newspaper. Life is so peaceful, viewed from above, and we only ever see a tiny part of life's architecture, if anything at all.

I float closer and see my reflection through the sunlit window; perfectly rounded golden leaf, lost all body fat without a faddy body wrap.

The boy walks back inside to greet his father, leaving behind the perfectly neat garden.

Blue lights blazing, an ambulance arrives, breaking the silence. A whirlwind scatters the perfect pile of leaves as the paramedics run towards the creek, and I wish I could do more than just weep. I want to see; deep in the water, in the white mist, is me. There goes my body in a blue bag, under a sheet, loaded into the ambulance behind the creek.

The neighbours pull down their blinds, but the little boy peeks through to give me one last wave. I'm an anonymous, euphoric, thin, golden leaf. Never afraid of the storms that are guaranteed to blow me away. A light of consciousness grew on me as my mind found its peace. I am now part of the sky and love skimming in the wind, in an unaltered and primal world of nothing but happiness and free, golden leaves.

Writing competitions with story prompts

This 500-word maximum writing challenge prompted writers to use the following words: 'star,' 'war,' 'force' or 'something that flies.' Here is a sample entry:

'Letters in the Snow'

A long time ago, when I was ten years old, I sat by the fireplace listening to a monotonous story told by my grandfather.

As I'm lighting a candle on his grave and looking at the tiny blob of flame pulsing in the melting snow, I recall a memory that will never drain away, like melting snow around a graveyard.

"The sun set early, light fading away… " he says as if to symbolise the dark forces coming. "Rapid gunfire behind the tall birch trees, cold bitter air biting chunks of my cheeks, fresh blood drops on the snow, bits of letterhead flying in the air, envelopes shredded to tiny bits, landing next to my warm brown leather boots, half a human finger, followed by a clavicle bone… all shattered around the snowy path made by the potent landmine." He takes a sip of water to clear his throat before continuing. "My horse had bolted a long way back and I only had the waning moonlight to guide me along." He pauses as the oaky smell of the fire penetrates the room. I'm considering backing away towards the living room where the others are watching a film. The volume goes up: *"Maverick, you just did an incredibly brave thing. What you should have done was land your plane!"*

I twist my hair around my thumb and fiddle with the chewing gum that's been stuck there forever. I think of that horse. And then, looking at his haunted eyes sparks a change in me; I see his depth as a human being. The procrastinating ten-year old child suddenly becomes extremely decisive. I'm staying put and listening to my grandfather's story instead of ducking out to watch Maverick fly in 'Top Gun.'

"I moved slowly in the snow, but I imagined being a flame, no one can touch it." He continues with a cracked voice, caught in his throat, eyes fixated on the fire slowly dying in the fireplace. "I tried to protect the army-issued postal bag with my life. It was heavy, full of letters. My role was a very important one, to give soldiers hope." His voice shrinks. He slowly picks up a poker with his wrinkly hands and stirs the ashes. A wisp of grey smoke curls through the air as I yank the rest of the chewing gum out of my hair with great force. "Do you want me to get some more firewood?" I interrupt.

He shakes his head politely and continues, "The deepest footprints in the snow, the stars still shining bright in the dark sky, the fighter planes dropping bombs, flying above our beautiful land, war ships sinking in the ocean." He exhales and looks me in the eye. The music gets louder in the living room. Maverick's fighter jet seems to have landed safely as the tiny blob of flame fades away in the fireplace.

Writing scholarship applications and introductions

Here is a short example of how you can get started writing various scholarship applications. It is important to give well-rounded, positive answers outlining your personal interests with career goals. Keep your answers short and keep in my mind the outcome you want if you receive the scholarship.

Scholarship application sample for travel writing

Winning a world-class scholarship would mean that I am on the right path, doing what I love, and able to connect with talented, inspiring people. It would also give me added confidence, as I would be completing a very important task and taking on the responsibility of creating a foundation that will allow me to get closer to my career goal of being a travel writer.

My mixed cultural background contributes to my intense love for travel, cultures, writing, communication and different languages. I am an adventurer, but also a life-long learner.

In January, I finished my Diploma for Advanced Professional Writing and Editing with High Distinction. I also have a BA in Media and Society, and an MA in Art, Design and Visual Culture.

I speak more than one language fluently and have studied Spanish for many years.

I am able to open my mind and transfer my thoughts to paper in various places, whether in a busy café or during the peacefulness of a train ride.

The main thing for me is being able to harvest ideas from life around me. I am inspired by life and I write from a place of excitement and energy.

I'm unique, dedicated and I can overcome obstacles. I never shy away from an opportunity to step outside of my comfort zone to seek new and inspiring writing experiences that help strengthen my work.

Creative prompts and practice dialogue

Here are some prompts for a story idea and how to start creating scenes:

New College. No parents. New friends. One wild party. Ocean. Missing girl. One weekend to find her.

    Themes: vampires, magic
    Readership: young adult
    Outline of the characters:
    Elora: main character
    Ellen: mother of Elora
    Tamandra: Elora's new friend
    Mrs Verona: school maiden
    Melody: nasty bully
    Jay and Santos: two boys at school
    Lon: the boy that everyone likes
    Jerome: the weird guy who holds a party in his room
    Yakov: Elora's grandfather in Russia

The scene prompt:

- Characters move to a boarding school, find new friends and go to a party
- Fun is replaced with tragedy when one of the girls (Melody) goes missing in the ocean
- Melody had gone to the beach with Lon. Lon's two friends were on the beach drinking earlier and they all go swimming
- Melody swims in the ocean. Elora goes in after her but can't find her
- They go back to the halls of residence, but can't tell Mrs Verona what happened because they were all drinking and would get kicked out of the school
- Elora tries to contact her mother but can't get hold of her
- Elora reads in her mother's diary about Yakov, her grandfather in Russia, and decides to ask him for help
- What if Melody swam in the dark to the shore, walked up to the hill and fell down and hit her head?
- What if she is lying between the rocks when they find her and Yakov brings her back to life?
- Or is the witches drum going to help them find her?

Story dialogue

"So that's it? You can't stay here and I can't go with you?" I ask mother. "I want to be part of it somehow…"

I'm almost begging her. I thought of all those times she used to let me in to her secrets and show me how to spin her Nordic witches drum and let me touch our expansive collection of herbs, crystals and voodoo dolls.

"You have a talent and you need to study," she says firmly.

"I mean what I said, I want to go with you," I insist. "When will I see you again?"

"After the break. I will be back, I promise. This is something I need to do."

Mother looks peculiar as she waves at the lady at the top of the stairs, with short, dark hair and expensive pearls around her neck. I can smell her musky scent lingering in the air.

"This is Mrs Verona," Mother says.

"Elora." She nods, whilst standing tall and powerful within the amazing architecture of the old building, featuring banquet halls and several large rooms.

I give her half a smile and whisper to my mother, "Ok. I'll let you go, on one condition."

She shakes her head, smiling, and flicks her large black sunglasses down from on top of her head.

"You promise to tell me all about Dr Odugo and the spells…"

Mother suppresses a sigh. Once again I slipped something out of my mouth without realising, so I say loudly, "Have a good holiday, Mum!"

She reaches out to hug me and I look down to the ground for comfort.

"The delivery company will bring your boxes this afternoon." She bites her lip and I can tell she is trying not to cry in front of Mrs Verona.

"I will call you as soon as I land in Nigeria. Have fun, make some new friends," she motions towards a girl with a purple balayage hairstyle slowly walking past us blowing a pink gum.

"Tamandra!" Mrs Verona says in a chilly voice.

The girl turns on her heels, giving me a cheeky wink and walks fast towards Mrs Verona.

"She looks like fun," Mother says, sensing my frustration. We smile, giving each other one last tight hug.

As I watch her leave and wave goodbye, the green surroundings look so peaceful. I can see the window of my new room, facing the cricket ground.

Mrs Verona's voice startles me. "Elora, Tamandra will show you to your room."

I follow Tamandra up the stairs and she hands me the key. "I almost forgot, we are having drinks in Jerome's room, number fifteen, on your left," she motions towards the end of the dark corridor.

"Sounds awesome, thanks so much," I smile at her.

The dead silence of the small room greets me, but I don't want to run from my life. It is time to find my own spark of excitement. I want to meet souls full of beauty, underneath the social wall we all have to climb. People like my mother, who chooses to shine even after all the storms she's been through.

I glance at my watch and open the window. For a moment I study my reflection before looking down at the cricket ground. A boy with brown curls hanging down his forehead is slowly walking across the field, his hands in his pockets, looking down at the ground as if he has lost something. As I watch him leap over puddles, there's a knock on the door. My boxes are here. I quickly unlatch the door. The delivery man looks as if he can't wait to drop the boxes one by one as quickly as possible.

I rush back to the window, but the boy on the cricket field has disappeared.

I crouch down for the cardboard boxes.

"Well… " I say with a sigh, "these aren't my boxes. All of this belongs to Mum."

I lean across the boxes and yawn, "Life's little jokes… " before I start ripping one open.

I need something to wear, especially if I'm going to the party tonight.

For a moment the room smells like a rose garden as I pick spilled potpourri out of the box.

I pull out a red cashmere jumper and a green floaty dress. There is a much-used, red hard-cover journal wrapped inside the dress.

I turn the pages and neat writing stares back at me as if to invite me to look deeper into the book's secrets. I turn a page and it reads "Choose to be conscious, and you will see the truth." A recipe for a "Cup of Good Juju" reads: apple cider vinegar, turmeric, hot water and lemon…

I knew Mother never danced with a wine glass like other mothers; she was either concentrating on her spells or taking long walks in graveyards.

I turn the page and read;

"It's weird because I felt like I could kill them, and I never had those feelings before. It was just me and Elora, and a lot of anger."

A knock on the door startles me and I drop the journal. I left the door ajar and Tamandra peeks in. "You look like you have lot of secrets."

I stare at her, questioning me like she is, mastering the art of timing.

"Your little rose garden," she inhales the potpourri and carefully steps around the pieces scattered on the floor.

"If we are going to be friends, you have to share things," she says, her eyes darting left and right. She picks the book up off the floor and starts reading with acid in her voice:

"*After all these years I gathered the courage to follow his black Bentley. As his driver opened his door, I instantly recognised the same Saville Row tailored suit and full-leather heirloom briefcase. Yakov, had not changed a bit.*

I stood in the corner of the cobblestone street, watching the lights come up, revealing a large grandioso apartment room. A tall man stepped out of the shadows, his eyes gleaming red with power, his pale, almost transparent skin showcasing blue veins. I stood in silence where I was, I didn't know what else to do. Blood vessels twisting in his face, I almost expected him to move his chalky body closer to his bodyguard and start feeding off him, sinking his teeth into his neck.

"Don't kill him," I whispered under my breath, thinking he was fighting the urge to feed.

His lips twisted into a smile and I saw a flicker in his gleaming eyes. I've heard all about Mafia bosses having violent tempers, but despite his tough appearance, he seemed different.

I kept looking up, my expression turning into a slow smile. And so everything I'm keeping inside comes rushing to the surface.

The bodyguard poured him a glass of expensive whiskey, and I almost heard the glasses click in the cold night as they toasted something. I chose to believe we were not the 'feeding from people' type of vampire. We have no blood dripping down our fangs, no urge to feed on anything but normal food, no weakness in the sun; summoning and dream-walking is all we can do. Maybe this will change, who knows? Are we eternal beings? Only time will tell. We don't live under a blood red moon in the eternal night time. My belief is that there are people like me walking around all over the place, they just don't know they have such powers, remaining as naive as I was."

I roll my eyes and she stops reading.

"We can't talk about it... " I motion at the diary.

"What did I say before? Oh… that we can't be friends if you don't share…"

"It's just that some friends, once you get to know them, end up sucking the life out of you…"

"Like vampires. Emotional vampires, Elora. So do tell…"

"Can you please promise not to tell anyone?"

"Your secret is my secret. People have to share things sometimes." She is trying to convey some compassion in her voice.

"I've been embracing what Mother does rather than questioning it, because that's the way it has always been. She has voodoo dolls too, and crystals. A lot of people have those, right?"

Tamandra nods and sinks inconspicuously into the worn Ikea futon. "Well, not so sure about voodoo dolls, but carry on…"

"Tragic things happened in her life early on, and it didn't get any better when she met my father. Anyway, all this must have made her delusional and rather than accept her cruel reality, she filled her imagination with –"

"Why didn't you tell someone who could have helped her? I mean, it would suck to be a vampire… get it" she winks with laughter.

"There is no treatment for clinical vampirism."

"Yeah I guess not. My father went to see a psychologist because he was exhausted with work and they told him to write a book or go for a swim! He works as a baker, he can hardly write a sentence and I've never seen him near the water… I mean, would swimming stop your urge for blood?"

"Tamandra, she's not compelled by bloodlust. It's her imagination, messed up because of what happened to her."

"I think having that sort of imagination would be cool. Maybe there are more people with Edward Cullen syndrome?"

"Since I told you all this, could you help me with something?"

"Let's bite on it!" she laughs. "Sorry, there are so many vampire jokes. And I mean, Edward Cullen was kind of cute, but creepy."

My eyes fixate on her hair. "Tamandra, you don't have any secrets? That's why your hair is so big and purple, because it's full of secrets, right?" I smile at her and she laughs.

"Well, nothing like your mother's Edward Cullen syndrome…"

"Let me guess... talking about Edward Cullen, you like a boy at school?"

"Maybe," she looks down at her nails.

"Tell me who. Come on!"

"No."

"About your mother... maybe she's just treading in her own natural world. Our world has domesticated her and controlled her mind. She's not rebelling and acting on her bloodlust. She's taming thousands of years of indoctrination." She eyes me with determined composure, the pink flush on her cheeks disappearing.

"Her alien religion, if you can call it that... and her foreign birth will always separate her from everyone else," she pauses. "Do you think having those thoughts is painful for her, or is she in peace with her natural, organic self?"

"That's deep, Tamandra. You will definitely succeed in this college. You know, I grew up burying voodoo dolls at graveyards with her. You may have played with Barbies, but I played with voodoo dolls. That was normal to me. My natural, organic self... "

Tamandra pulls her phone off her pocket, "I'm just going to google something"

"Listen, she hasn't bitten anyone, if that's what you're looking for. No murders, no mayhem," I say.

"The powerful blend of human and vampire blood! That's it! Have you not ever thought that she could actually be a real vampire, but half human?" she questions me, retaining her steely composure.

"No, just simply transferring trauma into a story – in her head."

"Look, let's have a look at her journal. There must be something we can bite on."

"Bite on?"

"Very funny, Tamandra... " I sigh.

She reaches to pick the journal up off the floor but I jump in and kick it away from her, regretting telling her anything.

"No. Just leave it. I don't know why I opened up to you."

"You opened up to me because you don't want to fear your own memories by holding on to them. Playing with voodoo dolls as a kid, come on! My super power is resourcefulness. I can help you. You just have to trust me. I can tell you've never trusted anyone and now I know why, because of your mother."

The slamming of a neighbour's door startles me and I look down at my watch.

'Let's go to this party?" I ask her, my tone softening.

"Yeah. I guess I can unlock the mystery of your mother's journal later."

We shut the door behind us and make our way to the party. The music is getting louder and chatter fills the dark corridor of the halls of residence. Jerome's door keeps opening and shutting as people push in and out.

Tamandra nods excitedly as we make our way to the drinks table.

"What's that?" I ask her as she scoops bright red drink out of a bowl with plastic cups.

"I don't know. Energy drink with alcohol?" she laughs at the obvious. "Live a little."

She passes me the unappealing drink mixture.

I take it, but as soon as she turns, I set the cup on the table.

The boy with brown curls makes an entrance and dead silence falls upon the room.

Tamandra's eyes beam excitedly. Downing the drink in one go, she whispers, "That's Lon. Isn't he gorgeous… so hot!"

I smile and say, "Go and talk to him."

"I don't think I need to, he's coming this way. I think I'm going to faint," she says a little bit too loudly.

He gives us a curious look as he walks over.

"I haven't seen you before," he says, lowering his eyes and flashing his perfect white teeth.

"Elora. I just moved into the halls today."

"Nothing as fun as the halls," he says. "I'm Lon, by the way."

Tamandra is already on her second or third drink and steps closer to him, ignoring me.

"Your hair looks great. How did you get it that colour?" he whispers to her.

Tamandra's eyes light up. "It helps me to stand out." She turns her head away as her cheeks turn pink, slowly ripening to bright red.

He grabs a drink and walks off to the dance floor.

"Can I guess what your secret is? Brown curls?" I lower my eyes at her, mimicking Lon. "Easy. It's Lon, isn't it?"

She shrugs in response, the pink flush slowly rising in her cheeks, making her look more innocent.

"Everyone has a crush on Lon," she leans back, maintaining a glorious silence, staring at the dance floor. She's clenching her fists as if she is being defeated in the game of love.

I start pushing her over to the dance floor.

"You can't force me to… "

I keep on pushing and she stumbles, her drink spilling, and has no choice but to dance.

Lon turns and moves closer to her, and in a few seconds the two of them are dancing together, smiling.

Lon takes her arm and spins her around.

Coming across so many faces on the dance floor, I lean against the wall and observe the energy flowing between them.

I have never been on a date, not without Mother hovering protectively behind me. I wonder what it would be like as I observe Lon's cute brown curls falling down his face.

Tamandra rolls her eyes at me, before drowning in Lon's.

Their perfect moment comes to an abrupt end as a girl wearing a pair of canvas shoes and a short, white mini skirt pulls Lon away from Tamandra, leaving her standing there, embarrassed. The girl gives Lon a drink and laughs hysterically. She looks like she has had more than a few glasses of that red punch.

I quickly wave my hand at Tamandra.

"Hey!" I yell, and she walks towards me.

"You didn't need to let him go like that."

"She literally stole him from me!" Tamandra fumes defensively.

I glance towards the dance floor. The girl and Lon have disappeared.

"That's Melody. She's come to ruin my life."

"Do you know her?"

"Yeah. She's a bully and no one can touch her. That's the disconcerting truth."

"Well, a drunk bully. She practically kidnapped Lon," I say, staring at the dance floor, at a loss as to where Lon might be.

"Should we go and find him?" I ask.

Tamandra doesn't look like she wants to think it over. She grabs my arm and we walk outside as fast as we can.

"Let's find *them*," her words come out determined.

As we walk across the cricket field, the grass feels a little wet and the earthy smell fills our nostrils.

"What if they are actually seeing each other and now Melody is angry at me?" she says, sounding a little worried.

I try to pull her from her thoughts. "Let's just find them. I think that drink at the party wasn't doing anyone any favours…"

"I feel a bit sick actually," she holds her stomach as we almost run across the field.

"Do you want to stop?" I ask her as we hear a loud, agonising scream.

The voice echoes through the night. Something is not right.

"I think someone needs help."

Tamandra holds her stomach tighter and kneels over on the grass.

"That did sound like someone in distress…"

"There's a short cut to the beach on the left," she motions, the dark night falling on us.

"You go," she says as I glance behind me and start running towards the beach.

"Lon! Melody!" I yell louder as I get to the edge of the shore.

I hear a girl scream again and I run faster. When I get close enough to the sear, I see an arm waving in the water. I'm not waiting around.

I pull my jumper off and leave it to be washed up on the beach. It's too late to see the rip current and seaweed moving away from the shore. Like a powerful force to be reckoned with, the discoloured water, caused by sand and other sediment picked up by the narrow current traps me. I swim parallel to the shore and manage to get back to the playful and pretty shallow waters. Holding my breath, my heart skips a beat as I squint into the patches of darkness that hover just beyond the shoreline.

"Elora!" Tamandra's squeaky voice echoes across the sand dunes, but I can't see anything.

I lift my exhausted head up and wave, seaweed stuck in my hair.

"Over here!" I yell as loudly as I can, but my voice is not carrying very far.

"Elora!" she yells again.

I stand up, the cold ocean breeze wrapping around me. She runs towards me, "My god, where is Lon?"

Tears race down my cold cheeks. "I think I saw Melody in the water… I tried…"

"Let's get out of here," she whispers.

The waves carelessly drooling onto the sand, we start walking.

Tamandra is resisting the urge to wipe tears from my cheeks. A clump of my hair topples over my face as I start coughing.

She is gently patting me on the back as we keep on walking faster.

Ahead of us in the golden gritty sand among the broken shells lies Lon. Beside him are his belt, crinkled trousers and shirt. His chest still heaving, we lift him up. A tall and powerful figure stands on the dark beachfront where green grass is bending over the sand dunes. I try to see the face. I can make out a grin right before the figure shifts, heading to the left, towards the woods.

"Did you see that?" I elbow Tamandra.

She shakes her head and I turn my head back to the water. The darkness feels like every last star in the galaxy has died.

The next morning, I slowly pull myself up in bed. The sun is peeking through the curtains, and Tamandra brings me warm lemon tea in a pink china cup.

"Drink up."

"I didn't drink that red punch at the party."

"I did, and I regret it," Tamandra says.

"Have you been here all night?"

"Yes, after we took Lon back to his hall. He looked like he needed to sleep it off."

I sneeze, spilling the tea. "I hope I'm not getting sick." I sniff my damp hair that still smells of seaweed.

"I've been reading something while you were sleeping."

"And you hung up my wet clothes! How nice of you." I stare at the green dress on the hanger.

Tamandra looks at me with a cynical smile.

"Your mother's journal…"

"No, you didn't. Can you not?" I place the teacup on the floor.

"It's too enticing. I can't stop reading it. Her life has been a rollercoaster of emotions and crazy people."

"Thanks for keeping an eye on me, but…" I twist my sticky, damp hair, facing the stacks of moving boxes spread around the messy room.

Suddenly something stirs inside me. I close my eyes and feel the ravishing waves on my skin.

"The drunk girl from the party. Where is she?"

"Oh, you mean the kidnapper? To be honest, I don't know why I even care… she just stormed on us and took Lon…"

"Yeah I remember that, but did she ever come back from the beach?"

"Lon didn't say anything. She might be with him as we speak," Tamandra says, as if she is coming to terms with the idea that Lon might be interested in someone else.

"Ok. Today you feel broken, but tomorrow you could be his everything. You never know. If we go searching for Melody, it might draw you closer to him, or him back to Melody…" I say. "The best we can do is try to get this situation under control. Let's find out if she is back."

"And if she isn't?" Tamandra looks worried.

"Plenty of reasons why she wouldn't be back, other than she was swept away… she could be faking it. Or she could have carried on drinking and partying with other people."

"Let's just be casual about this, not a big deal," she agrees, as we close the door behind us.

We walk up the narrow staircase and knock on the electric blue door.

Nothing. I knock again.

"Melody," Tamandra coughs, her face scrunching up.

"She's not back," I say, disappointed.

"Or she's been with Lon the entire night?" Tamandra's jealousy strikes again.

"Let's go and find out, then." I step back from the door.

We weren't going to wait in the shadows of the dark corridor quietly.

"Lon. Wake up!" We bang on the door.

"Ok, he's not here. Let's just forget about everything and go," Tamandra says.

As we are about to turn on our heels, the door slowly opens.

Lon's tired face peeks out. "I was sleeping."

"Is Melody here?" Tamandra storms in as if he has been cheating on her all night.

Two of his friends sit on the couch, about to burst into a laughing fit.

"No, I haven't seen her since the beach."

"So you were the last person to be seen with her?"

Lon shakes his head, confused, as his friends pretend to cough but can't stop laughing.

"She could have just gone somewhere else to party," I suggest.

"Did she take her clothes off?" Tamandra fires at Lon, you can see the jealousy bouncing off her eyes.

"You mean, did she leave them on the beach," I try correcting her, as Lon's friends laugh in the background. I give them a deadly stare, but deep down in all that laugher lies the agony of their hangover from last night.

"What do you want me to do, go to the police?" Lon stands right in front Tamandra. She takes a step back and sighs.

"And you two, what's so funny?" she locks her fuming eyes on Jay and Santos.

"Look, it was two in the morning, it was quiet and peaceful on the beach, except for Jay and Santos, drinking and singing. That's why we went there in the first place, to hang out with them," Lon says.

"So, you two want to tell me your side of the story?"

"It was too claustrophobic at the party. All those people in that weirdo Jerome's small room, packed in like sardines, drinking and dancing. We went to the beach to drink and asked Melody to come with us. A walk on the beach would have cleared her head," Santos says in a deep voice.

"She said she was going to dance first and turn up there later," Jay continues. "Lon passed out on the beach and Melody went for a swim."

"What happened next?" Tamandra fires like a seasoned detective.

"Well, to be honest, it was like a hallucinatory adventure with swirling colours all over the sky… I was too drunk to remember," Jay says.

'That punch at the party… was one of the most potent drinks I've ever tasted," Santos concludes.

"So, you two drunks don't remember anything else? When did you leave the beach?" Tamandra demands.

"I think we stumbled on the rocks somewhere before heading back."

"Why are you worrying about her, anyway?" Jay asks.

"We heard someone scream, like an agonising scream. Elora thinks she saw Melody in the water."

"Why don't we just wait? I mean, we can't get Jerome into trouble for the drinks. He would get expelled. And probably all of us, if it's up to Verona," Lon says. "She would literally drive us all to the station and say, "It was nice knowing you, knew you were going to ruin your lives from the start," then let out an evil laugh and play with her expensive pearls."

"We can't go harassing people about her, just let it be," Jay agrees with Lon.

"So, you guys were the last to be seen with her and now you want to act like you had nothing to do with it?" Tamandra fires again.

"We don't have to analyse everything and make it a worst-case scenario. All we are trying to say is that we should wait and see if she returns."

"Tamandra, Melody always ignored you and you said she was a vile bully. She's probably just ignoring all of us and has gone somewhere. Stop stressing," Lon shrugs.

I look at my phone. It's been 34 hours since Mother left and I have not received a message from her.

"I have things to do," I say. I'm starting to agree with the others as I walk towards the door.

"Wait, what?" Tamandra puts her hands on her hips and waits for an answer.

"I have to go. I'm sorry. I'm sure she will come back today"

Later that afternoon, back in my room, Tamandra is 'welcoming the day' with a sun salutation pose. I've never seen her face so determined. "Today we will find Melody."

"It's been too long…" I sigh. "I don't think it was her screaming, or in the water."

"Always the optimist. Luckily I got someone to help us."

"I don't think the boys will be much help," I shake my head.

"I wasn't talking about the boys," she smirks and peeks through the curtains at the cricket ground.

"Look," she motions to the field.

I reluctantly get up and pull the curtain. A large black car is parked right outside the window. There is a knock on the door.

I open the door and nearly die. He is here, after all these years. Mother would *literally* die. All the puzzle pieces Mother put together to work out who he is. I wish she were here. He is smiling, because he clearly wanted all of this to work out, without danger and secrets.

I wonder if you knew what I looked like, like I always wondered about you, but here you are, right in front of me, unexpected.

"Elora," he says with a husky voice, twisting his head to the left.

I roll my eyes and don't know where to look. All my life, and Mother's life, we thought about you. I'm breathing slowly and taking a step back without saying a word.

"How did you do this?" I whisper to Tamandra under my breath.

"Remember when I was googling stuff on my phone?"

God no, she is too obsessed.

Even in his old age, Yakov has a killer smile. No wonder Grandmother was weak at the knees.

"You broke my grandmother's heart," I swallow.

"It was long time ago, Elora," he says with his strong Russian accent.

"I want you to remember who you are, Yakov," I say, still in daze.

"Who I was. Not anymore, Elora. It was another life."

"How about you talk about this later and help find Melody?" Tamandra coughs behind me. "What if someone has her, some vicious monster, and you two are here talking about history? History of human affairs."

"It's just surreal, Tamandra… "

"Why don't we take a walk to the beach?" Yakov interrupts. "And you two can tell me everything that led to this."

"Everything?" Tamandra says. "Yes sure. Well, we all got drunk."

"No *we* didn't," I correct her.

"Ok, well *you* didn't," she gives me a look.

"If you want me to help, I need to know how she ended up in the water."

"Well I'm not sure if it was her in the water… or anyone at all." We walk across the hall. Not a sound can be heard through the hallways.

Lon's door opens and he joins us. Out of the corner of my eye, I see Tamandra locking eyes with Lon so many times, I don't think anyone can come between them now.

People are crowding around Melody's door, but as we walk past, they all separate, looking down and avoiding eye contact with any of us.

As we walk to the beach, Yakov locks his eyes on the ground.

"I'm so sorry we didn't have the best start… " he sighs heavily.

"You made the wrong choice," I snap.

"I had to live with it all my life." Yakov tries to place a hand on my shoulder. "You are in no position to say that!"

"I know more than you think. All those lives ruined, Mother's health… " I bite my lip and stop before I say too much.

"I know you can't trust me," he says quietly.

When I touch his hand, I feel a cold vibration through me – like death. What if Melody is dead too?

"All I remember is that she said she was going for swim. She started to undress, so I turned around," Lon says.

"So you never actually *saw her* go into the water?" Tamandra snaps at him.

"No, I did not. I didn't want to see her stripping down to her underwear, so I turned around, and must have passed out. Last thing I remember is turning around, hearing the waves and staring at the night sky, the stars…"

"What did you talk about before she disappeared?" Tamandra tilts her head and eyes him up like a jealous girlfriend.

"She asked me if I thought you were prettier than her…" he lowers his eyes.

"And then she just decides to go swimming out in the ocean at night, by herself?" I interrupt.

"At the end of the day, you let her go in the water alone," Tamandra snaps at Lon again.

"She could have swum across to the rocks?" I ponder.

"Is there anywhere else you think she might have gone?" Yakov asks, standing behind Tamandra and staring down at Lon.

"She wasn't going to run away" Lon says and looks away.

I nod and add, "Let's try and find her clothes. She might have had a handbag with her."

We scatter around the sunny beach, searching. It's the weekend, so the beach is full of people.

Near the rocks, under some sand, I see a familiar, scrunched-up top.

I pull it off the sand and underneath is Melody's purse. I dig it up and wipe the stuck sand off it.

"Over here!"

"Well, she didn't take anything with her," I conclude, and like wolves we gather together on Moon Pool beach and chant our rescue plan.

"She must still be here," I whisper, staring at Yakov for some kind of clue.

He is looking over at the rocks and scratching his nose.

"The rocks?" I ask.

"How about you walk in that direction, Elora," his gaze tells me he knows something.

I nod and start walking off.

And, there she is.

I get to my knees and lean over her. She is unresponsive.

"She's here! Melody is here!" I cry, not wanting to rush back to the crowds on the beach.

Suddenly Yakov stands next to me, looking down at Melody's wounds and holding a phone to his ear. I wonder if the scent of blood made it possible for him to find her so quickly. He is scratching his nose again and I wonder if the scent also makes his nostrils flare. The wind gently blows salty air from the crystal blue ocean and he kneels down next to me.

"Her body must have been through some cold temperatures at night," Yakov whispers as he waits on the phone.

He starts talking to the operator and I glance over at the crystal clear water before holding Melody's cold hand. I imagine her diving into the water at night, splashing freely, fish swimming around her, ending up here with a pale blue face and cracked lips. She had let the current take her, not realising how close to the rocks she was.

III

WORKSHEETS

Worksheet 1 – Identify and discover you; examine your habits and connect with your writing

1. List three or more things you did this morning (what kind of clothing did you choose to wear and why, which fragrance did you spritz and why did you choose this one, the breakfast you had and other things you did)

1.

2.

3.

2. Describe three occasions you felt happiness. Where were you, with who and what were you doing? What did you look like? Your hair and your clothes?

1.

2.

3.

3. Write a short story about the last meal you cooked (describe the smell, the taste…) a book you read, a romantic night you had or a gift you gave to someone.

Worksheet 2 – Kickstart the creative writing process

This worksheet was created to help you to take action, be inspired, allow your imagination to run wild and help you to come out of the writing closet.

The first step is to print out and complete each section to map out your intentions, goals, habits, outcomes and accountability.

The second step is to create a routine that allows you to review your writing progress.

First of all, write down three activities that bring you the greatest sense of happiness, joy and peace of mind and give you clarity (I hope writing things down/journaling/storytelling feature here!)

1.

2.

3.

Now, write down three of your preferred writing categories (journaling, fiction, poetry, songwriting, screenwriting, short stories, travel writing, anything that makes you pick up the pen!)

1.

2.

3.

Write down your three main weekly goals regarding your writing (for example: at least one journal entry per week/brainstorm for a new short story idea/one finished poem by the end of the week).

1.

2.

3.

Worksheet 2 - Kickstart the creative writing process

Brainstorm ways you can be held accountable (self-responsible) for your writing and record how accomplishing a task makes you feel. Enforcing accountability plays a key role in success (such as emphasising the importance of the task for your wellbeing/ involving helpful people with authority). Use your current diary and write everything down in point form if easier.

List three things that the happy, prosperous, highly successful version of yourself would write about to attract readers and get your message out in the world

1.

2.

3.

Worksheet 3 – Observations and writing activities to help you overcome trauma

One of the most valuable resources as a writer is your ability to absorb the life around you. Develop and detail characteristics and feelings into your writing.

1) Take a walk around your neighbourhood or visit a beach or park and observe people, buildings, history, weather, nature, smell, colours or anything that conjures up memories or strong feelings. Write a short 300-word article on the feelings or impressions your outdoor trip evoked.

2) Go back to one recurring memory that makes you uncomfortable or sad, involving a person. Write a short dialogue with the person who caused you the pain. Try writing the conversation as a scene. This is an emotionally difficult task to complete. It doesn't have to be perfect, as long as you get the dialogue moving. Life begins outside of your comfort zone. Keep pushing yourself out of it and note your feelings after the writing process. This is when you start to attain true happiness!

Worksheet 3 – Observations and writing activities to help...

3) With this writing exercise, you are going to shift the negativity. Write a positive short story, poem or song based on a hurtful incident/insult you experienced. This could also be written in the form of dialogue, and you can practise different viewpoints (who is telling the story). If someone bullied you, shift the negativity by writing something positive. Feel-good stories, poems or songs make others feel happy. In this exercise, let go of fighting back and investing in the illusions of bullies and abusers.

4) Use your preferred writing form to explore the notion that 'what gives life meaning is the struggle that we live through' and let your writing flow. Be inspired!

Worksheet 4 – Character inspiration and dialogue practice

Whilst at university, I attended an acting course where we were taught a great technique that can be used in writing to explore not only your character, but the scene.

First of all, lie down in a quiet room, close your eyes and imagine your character in detail. How does your character feel when she/he is walking around in their apartment, childhood home or any place that comes to mind? Describe the surroundings, the air and the smell. Once you are at this stage, keep going further into their life and environment.

The next step is to write it all down.

If you plan on writing a long story, a character chart is a great way to give clarity to your story and bring your character to life.

In your chart, include the following and add more as you go further into the storyline:

Physical appearance in detail: age, prominent features, eye and hair colour, weight and height, distinguishing marks such as freckles or scars

Personality: strengths and weaknesses

Traits: motivations, introvert or extrovert, optimist or pessimist and accomplishments

Worksheet 4 - Character inspiration and dialogue practice

    Favourites: colour, music, food, films or books
    Background: hometown, childhood events, education, religion and finances
    Family: relationship with family members, birth order and relevance of any extended family members
    Habits and hobbies: when, how and why the character does something, such as yoga, sailing, travelling, painting, reading, having regular drinks with certain friends/co-workers

Finish these sentences in your character's voice:

I've survived a lot, including...

The coffee tasted bitter...

I'm strong enough to handle...

His skin was cold to touch...

Write a story that uses mainly dialogue (you can write it all in dialogue for practice, then create a short story or let it flow into a bigger project). Remember to build up to the story with background details and scenarios.

Final word

Documenting everything with transparency, honesty and vulnerability will help you to rise above personal difficulties to inspiration.

Going through abuse and hatred, I started to hate myself, my anxiety took over and I didn't want to go on. I wrote and reflected on my writing and decided this is not how my story will end. I now seek out the beauty and majesty of our world and I wish you the same success in your creative journey. There are stories all around us.

I hope these worksheets will give you the inspiration to take your writing further. Your personal story can be inspirational to someone else.

You don't need to be perfect to inspire others. Never underestimate what you can do, because how you deal with your imperfections and downfalls is your inspiration. You are a seeker of everyday magic for yourself, even if you never share your writing with others. You can become your own best friend. Let it all go, detach yourself and reflect on your writing. This was my turning point and allowed things to go in my favour. I was no longer suffering and my anxiety eased.

Sometimes in life, just like with the characters in our stories, something substantial has to happen to spark the change and alter the narrative. I hope you can write it out in some form, be it a poem, song, journal or exciting new novel. It will be a message, a light in the dark. You are in charge of not only how your character's personal story unfolds, but how yours does, too.

Final word

Writing helps you to reflect instead of react. You can learn from it and become a better person, because it can help you to open up and bring out the unafraid version of yourself.

I hope this book provides enough reasons why you should write and helps you figure out the 'how.' Use your conflicts to improve your life and don't let your previous inaction feed your fear.

Whatever life throws at you in the future, you can build resilience by responding creatively.

Every story has a struggle. Express it, gain positive perspective and rewrite the stars.

www.ingramcontent.com/pod-product-compliance
Lightning Source LLC
Chambersburg PA
CBHW020654300426
44112CB00007B/378